"An indispensable publication for all truly
dedicated beer drinkers and party animals."
—*The Villanovan, Villanova University*

"Absolutely fantastic!"
—*34th Street Newspaper, Univ. of Penn.*

"Good-natured madness."
—*New Orleans Times-Picayune*

"Destined to become the college student's bible."
—*The Vermilion, Univ. of S.W. Louisiana*

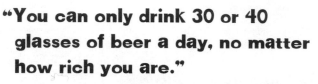

"You can only drink 30 or 40 glasses of beer a day, no matter how rich you are."

—*Col. Adolphus Busch*

THE COMPLETE BOOK OF BEER DRINKING GAMES

ANDY GRISCOM, BEN RAND, SCOTT JOHNSTON

Mustang Publishing
Memphis, TN • USA

PICTURE CREDITS: p. 7, John Mongillo/Jackson Newspapers; pp. 15, 19, & 109, AP/Wide World; pp. 16 & 18, Reuters/Bettman; pp. 17 & 31, UPI; pp. 48 & 49, David Ottenstein; p. 65, Rollin Riggs; p. 70, Earthwatch; p. 93, courtesy Heineken Breweries; p. 127, courtesy Universal Studios; p. 144, Rollin Riggs.

Drawings on pages 35, 38, 50, 63, 68, 78, 118, & 136 by SEAN KELLY.

No animals were harmed in the creation of this book. Unless you count brain cells.

Library of Congress Cataloging-in-Publication Data
Griscom, Andy, 1960-
    The complete book of beer drinking games / Andy Griscom, Ben Rand, Scott Johnston. -- Rev. ed.
        p.   cm.
    ISBN 0-914457-97-7 (alk. paper)
    1. Drinking games--United States. 2. Beer. 3. College students--United States Anecdotes. 4. United States--Social conditions--1980- Anecdotes. I. Rand, Ben, 1960- . II. Johnston, Scott, 1960- . III. Title.
GV1202.D74G75   1999
793.2--dc21   99-15569
                                                                                      CIP

Printed on acid-free paper.
10 9 8 7 6 5 4 3

*Dedicated to our parents,
for funding four years
of research*

DON'T BE STUPID

Alcohol is a dangerous drug. And, like it or not, it's an illegal drug in America if you're under 21.

Alcohol will severely impair your reflexes, and if you try to drive when you're drunk, you stand a good chance of killing yourself or murdering someone else. Here's a sickening statistic: Among people age 16-24, alcohol-related car wrecks are **the leading cause of death**.

Don't be stupid. Don't abuse alcohol. Don't drink and drive, and don't let your friends drink and drive, either. Use the designated driver system, or call a cab, or just crash on a convenient sofa.

Look, if you want to kill yourself, do everyone a favor and play with a toaster in the bathtub. Just don't drive drunk.

Acknowledgments

We had a great deal of help creating this book—both the original edition in 1984 and this revised edition. In particular, we would like to thank Harold and Lucille Morowitz for all their assistance and Eric Mogilnicki and George Shepherd for their excellent contributions.

We would also like to thank the following: Jake Jacobsen, Chris Jorden, Chris Cummings, Drew Lieberman, Pat Conran, John Garber, Charlie Clarke, Michael Clark, Andy Waugh, Mike Aubrey, Ray Small, Scott Gelband, Sarah, Jim, Fred, and Chuck Buffum, Bill Glynn, Sim Johnston, Dorothy Shaw, Ben Davol, Lawrence Callahan, Leo and Brian, Bart Enders, Joe Romano, Caitlin Doyle, Bruce Jacobsen, Rollin Riggs, Michel le Ventripotent, Mike Natan, Jake Smith, Malcolm MacLear, Loryn and Kim, Rich Smith, Ted Berenblum,  Whitney Sander, Doc-oh Burke, Bob Hallifax, Fred Loney, Dave Winans, Andy Kaplan, Dave Tohir, Todd Wadd, Gretchen Knapp, Steve Zuckerman, Mike Balay, George Johnston, Tom Hawkins, Mark Bolender, Telly Jorden, Lizey and El, Allison Christian, Mark Harris, Delta Kappa Epsilon, U. of Michigan School of Music, the Sumerians for inventing beer, Henry Ford for inventing the car, and Smith College for giving us an excuse to road trip.

CONTENTS

A SPECIAL INTRODUCTION TO THE REVISED EDITION

THE FUNNY THING IS, we don't remember ever deciding to write this book. We assume the decision came during a beery New Haven evening, but it's a memory forever lost, along with a few million brain cells. And while we were vaguely aware at the time that a book on drinking games was an amusing idea, we certainly had no idea what was to come. Hundreds of thousands of books sold. Two dozen printings and counting. A wildly successful sequel. Angry letters from college administrators and prudish Neo-Prohibitionists. Million-dollar movie offers. Tawdry affairs with Victoria's Secret models. The cover of *People* magazine—well, OK, we're getting a little carried away.

But one thing is certain. Nearly everyone who has attended college since 1984 has read, or at least heard of, ***The Complete Book of Beer Drinking Games***. Can Homer (the Greek poet, not Simpson) make the same statement? Can Faulkner? Can Proust? *Hmmmmm?* This is an awesome realization, when we bother to think about it.

And now here's the improved, thoroughly updated, ***Revised Edition***. To be frank, the whole thing seems like it happened a long time ago. Yet, certain events remain vivid: The first time we saw the book in a bookstore—and moved it to a better shelf position, while complaining to the manager that he had not ordered enough copies. (We might have been jerks, but we were *prophetic* jerks.) Our publicity tour in Florida during Spring Break. (We'll spare you the debauched details, but you can imagine what happened when we played Beer Hunter at 7:00 a.m. with the way-too-perky hostess of "Good Morning, Orlando.") The press conference at Rudy's, our favorite bar in New Haven, where we learned that reporters will cover *any* story if you promise free booze. Those were great times.

Now it's years later, and it's hard not to feel a little removed from our youthful phenomenon. You have to realize, we have actual *lives* now. Respectable lives, if you can believe it. Ben, a well-paid consultant, is married, owns a house near Boston, and has two children. Yes, he frets about how to tell them about the book when they grow up. (Once, we worried about what our mothers would think; now we worry about our daughters.) Andy is a doctor in Rhode Island, where he slinks around the halls of his hospital, hiding from the liver specialists. His professional advice does not include the virtues of chugging pitchers or swallowing quarters. Scott works in New York managing other people's money—*a lot* of other people's money. To his clients, he's a paragon of fiscal acumen—even though he eagerly quaffed half-full pitchers to win $3.75 during Slush Fund bouts just a few years ago.

Despite our adult status, we can't escape our past. Once, in a bar in Hong Kong, Scott happened to meet some Americans fresh out of business school. Someone mentioned the book and Scott's connection to it. "You guys are my heroes!" one of the students yelled. (Where *have* you gone, Joe DiMaggio?)

When Ben enrolled in Wharton, he thought he could sweep this beer games business under the rug. *I'm an adult now. Can't be associated with stuff like that,* he thought, hollowly. There was only one problem. He had included the book on his application, thinking it made him look "entrepreneurial." Early in the semester, the Dean gave a speech to the student body, praising the diverse accomplishments of the class. Wharton had students who had spliced genes, he said, students who had counseled the President, students who had started soup kitchens, etc. "One student," he added, "even wrote a hit book on beer drinking games!" Ben slumped in his chair as a wave of curiosity swept through the assembly. Then, one student—clearly an avid gamester—stood and pointed. "It's him! The beer games guy!" So much for adulthood.

We've concluded that we'll have to make peace with the fact that this literary achievement will always be out there, for good and bad. We will always be one of "those guys" who wrote that sick—but funny!—book on beer games. But that's OK, because we've gotten more out of the book than the book's gotten out of us.

Sadly, we must confess that we no longer spend our evenings playing Thumper and Beer 99. It's not that, in the abstract, we don't want to play or that we feel too mature to play. Rather, we've discovered certain physical constraints as we've gotten older—not to mention social and professional concerns. We still *feel* like the same guys who wrote the book, however. And there are moments when we happily regress. Sometimes it's a wedding, or an alumni function, or even a dinner party that brings us together from our far-flung homes. Oh, things start out respectably enough. But then one of us gets a wicked gleam in his eye as we gather 'round a table, and a voice, echoing a fondly remembered, simpler time, yells,

"What's the name of the game?!"

Andy Griscom Ben Rand Scott Johnston

Introduction:

A Few Words about Life, Love, and Beer

O nce upon a time, drinking beer was uncool, or, worse, "square." Smoking pot was "in" on college campuses in the 1960's and early 70's, along with Army fatigues, long hair, and minimal hygiene. The popularity of marijuana was really a matter of convenience for yesterday's youth (a.k.a. your parents): you could get high and make a political statement at the same time. Like Woodstock and rock music, smoking pot was part celebration and part protest.

But that's all passed. Our generation was oblivious to the problems of those years, being preoccupied with Little League and long division. Today, Vietnam is hungry for McDonald's and Diet Coke, and the flower children have grown up to become stockbrokers, advertising executives, and, in certain cases, President of the United States.

And, praise be, beer is back!

As we see it, the turning point was the presidency of Gerald R. Ford. Unlike his predecessors, Ford was a man you could imagine sharing a six-pack with. Lyndon Johnson invited defiance, from the burning of draft cards to the burning of joints. And Richard Nixon incited paranoia—it took a belt of hard liquor to get him off your mind.

But Jerry resembled your favorite uncle—perhaps not so

Billy Carter: the only brother of a President to have a beer named for him.

bright, but a certifiably good guy—and you just knew he could drink a beer. America's basic values, questioned by events here and half a world away, were beginning to reassert themselves. We began to feel proud to be Americans again, and we were happy to hoist a beer to Our Pal the President.

The true watershed, however, was the Carter Administration. Although Jimmy reminded many of milk of magnesia, what world leader has ever had a beer named after his brother? When the late Billy Carter created Billy Beer, he joined the pantheon of all-time great beer swillers, and it was clear that the golden nectar had re-entered the American mainstream. And Ronald Reagan, even though he was too old for a fierce round of Thumper, continued to show that beer was integral to the American Way (see photo on page 17).

Although George Bush never won any chugging contests, he was still a beer drinker's President, especially when he led the charge to kick Iraq's butt. For one thing, he had an appropriate

Our Pal the President: Gerald R. Ford, 1976.

last name. For another, he was in our fraternity, DKE. We <u>know</u> what he had to do in initiation. Trust us.

While the verdict is still out on Bill Clinton—would you want him on *your* Blow Pong team?—there are photos of him downing a brew, so perhaps there's reason for hope.

No regrets here: the resurgence of beer is a positive sign. Beer binds father to son, worker to worker, and student to student. Beer is American, not foreign, like drugs. Beer is the drink America comes home to, the drink of quittin' time, backyard barbecues, and nights out with the gang. Beer is for

Ronald Reagan hoists a cold one in a Boston bar.

before, during, and after the game—any game. Beer removes the agony from defeat and adds a thrill to victory.

And there's another great thing about beer: bars. In almost every town, from Portland, Maine to Portland, Oregon, places exist for only one reason: to create a pleasant environment for socking down a few frosties. Other things at bars—like peanuts, Monday Night Football, and jukeboxes—exist only to enhance the taste of that cold beverage in your hand.

But the absolute best thing about beer, as we will go to great lengths to prove, is that it can be used to play a lot of incredibly fun drinking games. These games have become the rage of young adult America, practically wiping out the existence of 8:00 a.m. college classes. In fact, we hoped this book would be distributed to all college students at orientation with other

After he finished this beer, George Bush decided to kick Iraq's butt.

essentials like course listings, school regulations, and meal contracts. Much to our surprise, every registrar we contacted flatly refused. (A few, however, did express interest in adding the book to their personal libraries.)

Of course, we do not advocate drinking beer to solve problems or escape from reality. We only argue that drinking beer can be fun and is, well, an honored American activity. After all, George Washington spent his spare time at Mount Vernon

Bill Clinton hoists brewage with Czech President Vaclav Havel.

brewing his own brand of ale.

In short, when America feels good about itself, it drinks beer, and drinking beer helps America feel good about itself. Enjoying the amber nectar by playing rowdy games is our generation's way of following that great American trait of going for the gusto in all areas of life. It is our hope that we have captured this spirit in the pages that follow.

**"We'll teach you to drink
deep 'ere you depart."
William Shakespeare, *Hamlet***

Beer Game Etiquette

To tell you the truth, beer game etiquette is a contradiction in terms. Beer games are often rude, and players even ruder. In an attempt to curb gross incivility, an altogether arbitrary set of rules has evolved among veteran gamesters.

Well, that's not really honest. The truth is, the more rules players must remember, the more infractions they make, and the more beer they drink. And this, after all, is the whole idea.

Beer game etiquette varies from one geopolitical region to another—indeed, from one game to another. There are, however, ten common rules players may invoke:

No Pointing. Since pointing is one of the most frequent acts, especially when identifying players who blunder, there naturally must be a rule against it. Anyone who points with his finger must take a swig from his beer. The only acceptable way to point is with a bent elbow.*

Gamesters may use only their elbows to point.

No Saying the Word "Drink." Whenever players use the word "drink" in any form (e.g., drinking, drinkable, drunk, drank, drinked, drinkly, etc.), they must drink—er, imbibe.

This practice originated with the game Whales Tails. Since whales don't have fingers, they must point with a flipper, assuming they want to point at something. When a human points with his elbow, it resembles a whale pointing with his flipper. Sort of.

Be sure to read "Beer Game Etiquette" to all players before you begin an evening of gaming.

 Wrong Hands. Right-handed players are forbidden to drink with their right hands, and left-handed players with their left. For the hard core, there is no drinking with either hand. When players infringe, they must drink again. Incidentally, it's poor sportsmanship to sit on your drinking hand or zip it inside your pants.

No Profanity. This needs no explanation, but it will drive you apeshit.

 The Ten Minute Warning. In addition to Rule #1, this is considered a standard regulation. Players must give a ten minute warning before quitting a beer game. This prevents a player who just lost big-time from shirking his penalties by claiming he hears his mother calling and dashing off, leaving the three pitchers he was supposed to chug.

No Pronouns. This is one of the most difficult rules. By excluding pronouns, players get confused when they try to identify each other. This makes them point, and so they violate Rule #1, and so they drink.

 First Infraction. If a player makes a mistake and the game continues for a while before players realize the infraction, any blunders after the original are nullified. Void where prohibited by law.

Discreet Digit. During a game, a player can discreetly hang his forefinger off the edge of the table. Players who see this quietly do the same as they continue to play the game. The last player to hang a digit drinks.

Golden Chair. Before a player leaves the game to go to the bathroom for a visit with Captain Leaky or for a casual reverse drink, he must say, "Golden chair" to gain immunity from being called while absent. This rule is crucial in verbal tag games in which players away on "business" often get called mistakenly.

Point of Order. Unless you are in the 8th grade (a.k.a. "the best two years of our lives"), you will rarely have parents around to supervise your beer games and make impartial rulings. So, the Point of Order establishes a tribunal to settle arguments, clarify rules, and make additions to a game. When a problem arises, a player should yell, "Point of order!" All players raise their elbows into the air and yell in response, "Point of order!" They then put their fists in the middle of the table with their thumbs sticking out sideways. The player who initiated the Point of Order states what the players are voting on—to introduce a new rule, for example, or determine whether Rufus may go to the bathroom. He then yells, "Vote!" and the players point their thumbs up for approval or down for denial. A denied motion must be accompanied by a loud buzzing sound by the whole tribunal, just like when the fat lady loses on *The Price Is Right*.

Essential Equipment

The Mung Rag

A **beer-gaming essential**, the mung rag is simply an old towel, bathrobe, or pair of boxer shorts used to wipe up the spills and, er, other secretions that inevitably occur during an evening of beer gaming. Hence, the mung rag's other name, the "table Zamboni." (A Zamboni, for those of you who grew up in the Third World or Texas and haven't seen much ice hockey, is the machine that glides around a hockey rink between periods, smoothing and re-surfacing the ice.)

To us, however, the mung rag is much more: it is our friend and trusted companion. One mung rag should last a full year. Never throw it away after a party. Rather, let your mung rag rest between beery bouts under your couch—or preferably under someone else's. Develop an intimate relationship with your mung rag, and let its unique aroma evoke the great parties past.

In olden times, Mung Rag Washing Day was a festive annual event.

If your mung rag should ever need washing—like when it attracts the attention of local health officials—place it, by itself, in an industrial-size washer with bleach, detergent, and antibiotics. Then run like hell.

Swill Beers

Since beer games require copious quantities of beer, the frequent gamester will want to use economical brands. After all, you just don't chug Samuel Adams. It's also a good idea to use beer that is at least remotely palatable. Enthusiasm for Thumper wanes quickly if the only brew you've got is a case of "Old Barleyfarts."

So here's a list of brands that we believe best combine economy and taste for gaming purposes: Old Style, Meister Bräu, Lone Star, Milwaukee's Best ("Beast"), Piels, Blatz, Schaefer, Ortlieb's, Rolling Rock, Rainier, Utica Club, Pearl, Dixie, Stroh's, Keystone, and Pabst Blue Ribbon.

Our favorite, however, is Black Label. (No, they're not paying us big bucks to say this.) Veteran gamesters call six-packs "Black Labs," and you can sometimes find it (warm) for about $6.00 a case. Calling cases of Black Label "kennels" is cool.

For our male readers, one last word about swill beers: At times, you'll want to play with a beer that doesn't even make the first gesture toward good taste (kind of like this book). You see, a beer that tastes really foul can make your games much more macho, because players get to prove to each other how much punishment they can take. We have found Wiedemann's, Old Milwaukee, Schlitz, Olde English 800, Stag, Colt 45, and Genesee Cream Ale particularly well-suited for this purpose. Imagine losing a long round of Beer Hunter with Genesee. Now that's *manly.*

Snarfing, Booting, and Reverse Drinking

Defining the Terms

Regurgitation is a delicate subject. No doubt there are those who prefer we not discuss it. However, we feel that if Oprah and Geraldo can talk about married transsexual midget cousins with tattoos on national television, we can discuss hurling.

Though there are many subtle variations and nuances in puking, three basic types concern us here: snarfing, booting, and reverse drinking. Each will be encountered from time to time by the beer gamester, so some clarification is in order.

Snarfing

A **snarf** is definitely undesirable. Snarfers have the odor of failure about them. Snarfing occurs when someone attempts to chug a beer—and fails. Usually, the unfortunate drinker pours beer into his mouth faster than he can swallow. As a result, the beer must seek an alternate exit, and much of it will find its way into the olfactory passages and out the nose. While spectators may find this amusing, it is, on the whole, an unpleasant and humiliating experience. *Advanced gamesters note:* A well-timed joke can induce a snarf in your opponents.

Booting

Booting is something with which we are all familiar. Commonly known as "throwing up," booting even happens to non-gamesters when they eat something nasty and get sick. Since it involves liquids and solids that have already begun the grand tour of the digestive tract, booting is by far the most wrenching form of regurgitation. Visual reminders of recent meals are often included as a bonus.

Reverse Drinking

Also known as "blowing foam," **reverse drinking** is the least unpleasant type of upchuck. Actually, it is a drinking tactic more than a drinking mishap, since it enables a player to continue beer-gaming long after his stomach says, "No." Simply put, reverse drinking is giving back to nature what you've just consumed. Ideally, the time between consumption and ejection (the "lag time") is precisely the time you need to reach a toilet. Unfortunately for bystanders, the lag time is often too brief for a player to run downstairs and find an empty stall. Reverse drinking is mostly painless and allows at least one more round of Boot-a-Bout or Blow Pong. Those with a scientific bent are fascinated to find that their recently imbibed beer is still foamy, while dieters appreciate all those rejected calories.

But Is There Deep Meaning in All This?

Something about drinking games brings out the best in a person—literally. You see, puking is a classic victim of bad press. Persistant negative publicity about blowing chow has created a vicious cycle: people don't look forward to ralphing, so they don't properly enjoy a good, vigorous barf. Let's consider some of the advantages:

The best thing about woofing is that it makes room for more beer. The advantage of this is self-evident.

Another positive aspect: Did you know that stomach muscles never get tighter than when you're booting? That's right, puking is great exercise! (Kind of gives you a whole new outlook on developing a "six-pack," doesn't it?)

A final attribute of yuking is that spawns great stories, which will make you quite popular at parties. What member

A lady-like ralph

of the opposite sex doesn't love a rousing tale about blowing doughnuts?

If you're still not convinced that booting can be a positive experience, consider the additional physical, spiritual, and philosophical reasons for joyously anticipating an occasional heave.

First, the act is, by definition, physically beneficial; your body responsibly decides (often when your mind is long past responsible decisions) against keeping that last beer.

Second, if you can free your thoughts of societal indoctrination, you'll realize that losing your lunch can be a transcendant experience. All at once, at a throne of porcelain, your body is poised in a moment of great catharsis. There is a sudden sense of complete abandon to a force greater than yourself, and then a profound quiet (and maybe a little spitting and coughing).

Finally, throwing up raises a timeless philosophical question. After a chunder, is your stomach half-full or half-empty?

Ten Places to Leave Your Lunch

1. mailbox
2. hanging plant
3. sock drawer *(not your own)*
4. glove compartment
5. laundry chute
6. dog bowl
7. fish tank
8. golf bag
9. freezer
10. through a sunroof *(either direction)*

The Boot Factor

(a.k.a. Earl Indicator, Ralph Rating, Vomit Vector)

The Boot Factor, using a scale of one to five, indicates the level of havoc a beer game will wreak upon your digestive system. The Boot Factor rates a game's capacity to stimulate a little-known area in the brain, the *regurgitus violentus loci*. A Boot Factor of 1 describes the lowest potential for tossing cookies, while a Boot Factor of 5 warns of an almost assured heave.*

However, the Boot Factor is more than just a guideline. Used wisely, it can provide essential pre-game information that you should use to plot strategy. For example, in a game with a low Boot Factor, concentrate on ways to defeat fellow players by using your intellect, such as it is. But after a few rounds of a high-Factor game, very little intellect remains, so players must focus on immediate physical concerns ("How big is my stomach?") and reserve thoughts on strategy for less cerebral matters ("Where is the closest toilet?").

For over-achievers, the Boot Factor provides a numerical incentive for consuming massive quantities of brew. Tell your bookworm friend that the Boot Factor can be compared to his G.P.A., with 5 being the *summa cum laude* of beer gaming. The knowledge that you are a regular upper-level competitor can do wonders for your self-esteem, not to mention attract countless fawning members of the opposite sex.

Use the Boot Factor strictly for comparison. Volume and frequency of gastrointestinal evacuations may vary with length of game and size of penalty. Your actual game mileage may be less. See dealer for complete details.

BOOT FACTOR ONE

Games rated Boot Factor One consist of a varied selection for the beginner who yearns for the excitement and camaraderie of competition, without the forced consumption of entire pitchers at a time. B.F. 1 games serve as an introduction, a preliminary step for the neophyte in quest of the upper echelons of beer gaming. For experienced players, Boot Factor One games can serve as limbering exercises for the more demanding contests to follow.

Indian Sweat
General Hover
Beer 99
Muffin Man
Burnout
Stack-a-Brew
Killer

Indian Sweat

Boot Factor: 1

Indian Sweat, the card game, is often played for money during a round of poker. But in **Indian Sweat: The Beer Game**, the stakes are much loftier, since players bet beer, not mere cash.

Each player receives one card face down. Players are not allowed to look at their cards. Instead, they must bring the cards to their foreheads without looking at their card's face. Thus, a player can see everyone else's card, but not his own.

Bidding commences. The dealer begins, and the rest of the players take turns betting any number of shots of beer that the card on their own forehead is the highest in the group.

As the "pot" increases, the players who feel their cards might be losers drop out. They must then drink the amount of beer in the "pot." At the end of the betting, the player with the lowest card must drink the final amount bid.

Tip: To represent graphically the total amount of beer wagered, the dealer can pour the "bets" into a pitcher in the middle of the table. Losers must drink an amount equivalent to whatever is in the pitcher.

"Now is the time for drinking, now the time to beat the earth with unfettered foot."
Horace, *Odes* **(23 B.C.)**

General Hover

Boot Factor: 1

Also known as "Hovering Bunnies," **General Hover** is so cute that even Barney and friends enjoy a round now and then.

The game begins with a "general hover"—all players hold out their hands palms down and shake them. One player initiates the action by clasping his hands and pointing at another player. The second player must then make Mickey Mouse ears. The player on "Mickey's" right must make a right-handed Mickey, and the player on his left must make a left-handed Mickey.

All three "Mickeys" must be created nearly simultaneously. Any player who delays must drink.

After holding these positions for a second or two, the player making the "full Mickey" says, "General hover," and every-

Even President Reagan enjoyed General Hover.

one begins hovering again. After a brief period, the Mickey clasps his hands and points to another player, who then becomes the new Mickey. This continues until someone messes up.

There is also a maneuver called the "jockey." Anyone may call for a jockey at any time during the game, except when players are Mickeying. During a jockey, players must jump up and slap their hands on their thighs, making a sound like a galloping horse. The person who initiated the jockey ends it simply by sitting down and announcing a return to "general hover." There is no point to a jockey except to make female players jump up and down and giggle.

Because **General Hover** is so cute, women seem to enjoy it more than men. Most guys we know wouldn't be caught dead making Mickey Mouse ears, unless of course they're trying to make "Mickey" with a nearby Minnie.

> **"My grandmother is over 80 and still doesn't need glasses. Drinks right out of the bottle."**
> **Henny Youngman**

Beer 99

Boot Factor: 1

In the Introduction, we implied that beer games build character. Well, not **Beer 99**. The object of this game is to lie, cheat, and steal your way to victory.

Beer 99 is a card game in which deception and sleazy tactics succeed, and honesty often fails. Each player receives four cards. The value of a card is the same as in blackjack: aces are worth one or eleven, face cards are ten, and all others are the card's face value. The first player throws one card face up to create a discard pile and announces the value of his card. The next player then plays a card and announces the sum of his card plus the first card.

The game continues in this fashion, with each player adding his card's value to the total. The object is to build the pile until it totals 99. When this happens, the person next in rotation must drink. If a player discards and sends the pile's value over 99, then he must drink. The cards are then shuffled if necessary, and the pile's value starts over at zero.

There are several ways to avoid topping 99. Kings, tens, and fours all have special properties. A king can give the total of 99 to anyone the player chooses. A ten increases *or* decreases the count by ten, so someone who gets 99 can play a ten and announce 89 to avoid drinking. A four allows you to skip a turn; if a player receives 99, he can play a four and pass the 99 to the next player.

A player must drink if he has no cards left and it's his turn to discard. To keep a full hand, a player should always draw after playing a card. The only time you may draw is immediately after you discard, so stay alert.

Now, about cheating. This is where most of the fun and skill appear in **Beer 99**. A good cheater will always have a large supply of cards in hand, shoe, sleeve, sock, etc. He can get them from anywhere, but the easiest place is from the draw pile. Deft players will also pilfer two or three cards from the

"99 to you, hosehead!"

discard pile or from fellow players. Players may also miscalculate the pile total as they discard.

The dealer, of course, has a prime opportunity to cheat. Simply deal one of the players—someone you'd really like to punish—an extra card. He'll think you screwed up to his advantage, and he'll keep the card. Then, at a critical juncture in the game, accuse this bozo of cheating! Give him a knowing wink just to rub it in—it's very satisfying.

If a player is accused of cheating, the others must vote on his guilt or innocence if the verdict isn't obvious. If more than half the players register "thumbs down," the accused must drink. Otherwise, all those showing "thumbs up" must drink for their false accusation.

Cheating infractions tend to increase as the game continues and alcohol obliterates your natural ethical inhibitions and all sense of integrity.

Muffin Man

Boot Factor: 1

Mother Goose will be turning in her grave when she hears about this one. But she won't be the only one who's spinning.

In **Muffin Man**, two players each balance a full cup of beer on their heads. They then must recite in unison a nurscry rhyme in loud, obnoxious voices. The first blockhead whose beer falls off not only gets wet but also must chug the victor's beer.

Somehow, we don't play this one a lot.

Burnout

Boot Factor: 1

Although **Burnout** requires a lit cigarette, even non-smokers can enjoy this game. In fact, many times we abstainers have bummed a cancer stick from some incredulous bar patron so we could play a few rounds. Smokers can't believe we use their precious butts this way. Tough.

The other equipment necessary to play is a dime, a glass (preferably short with a wide mouth), and a napkin. Put a single layer of the napkin over the glass and pull it down around the sides. Wet the napkin around the rim of the glass and tear off the excess, so the napkin covers only the mouth of the glass. The final setup will look like a miniature bongo drum. Next, take the dime and gently lay it in the center of the napkin. Now you're ready to begin.

Players take turns using the cigarette to burn holes in the napkin around the dime. Whoever burns the hole that causes the dime to fall must drink (from another glass, of course—we discovered that beer laced with ashes and burnt napkin really sucks). **Burnout** has a low Boot Factor because it can take an amazingly long time for the dime to fall. This, however, is why the game is fun. The dime often becomes suspended on an incredibly tiny strip of paper, and deciding where to burn the next hole can be a real challenge.

We highly recommend **Burnout** for the bar scene. You always make lots of new friends when you play, because everyone wonders what the hell you're doing and comes over to gawk. **Burnout** is also the perfect game to play when you're winding down after a night of intense beer gaming.

Stretch a napkin over the mouth of a glass.

Thirty Synonyms for "Beer"

1. brew	16. swill
2. brewski	17. pop
3. brewage	18. roadies
4. brew dogger	19. chilly
5. gold milk	20. stew
6. golden nectar	21. frosty
7. nectar of the gods	22. shooter
8. juice	23. toby
9. sauce	24. caker
10. goon	25. liquid courage
11. beevo	26. pounder
12. brew-hah	27. tweeners
13. suds	28. pony (8 ounces)
14. 12-ounce weight	29. green dragon
15. grog	30. screaming green meanies

Stack-a-Brew

Boot Factor: 1

Stack-a-Brew is the game to play on Saturday night with Friday night's empties, or Tuesday night with Monday night's empties, or... As you may have guessed, the idea is to take turns stacking cans as high as possible until they topple. It's really more fun than an Erector Set, or even Mr. Potato Head. The uncoordinated sap responsible for the crash must imbibe.

This game may be the beer drinker's version of a perpetual motion machine, because the more you play, the more equipment you have to play with.

Killer

Boot Factor: 1

In no way related to either Jerry Lee Lewis or **Kill the Keg** (a Boot Factor 5 game), **Killer** is another card game with drinking applications.

All players receive one card face down. One of these cards must be an ace, and the player who receives the ace is the "killer." His mission is to assassinate the other players one at a time by winking discreetly at each of them. He must not let anyone but his victim see the wink. Once a player has been "killed" by the wink, he declares himself dead and, to insure that he will rest in peace, he must chug his beer. Dying is always a dramatic event and involves moaning, clutching at the throat, and generally hamming it up.

If another player sees the assassin winking at someone else, he may accuse the "killer." If the accusation is correct, the "killer" must drink for each player left alive. The cards are then collected, and another round begins. If the accusation is false, the accusing player downs a penalty drink and promptly dies. But before giving up the ghost, he must also take his R.I.P. chug.

The Gamester's Glossary

alegar—Vinegar made from ale or beer. See also "mung rag aging process."

barm—The froth on beer. Also called *fob*. Fun to blow onto drinking buddies.

beer comb—A spatula used to scoop foam from the tops of beer glasses and mugs. Or, a cool way to style your hair.

bright beer—Beer separated from its dregs. Also called *racked beer*. (Dregs, the sediment in the bottom of a beer barrel, are also called *lees*.) Bright drinkers drink bright beer.

bunghole—The aperture through which beer enters a cask. The plug in a bunghole is called a *shive*. Hey, get your mind out of the gutter.

ferruginous—Beer that tastes as though it has a high iron content. Beer, like wine, has a variety of tasting terms, including austere, brackish, dank, flabby, skunky, swampy, and tinny. Our favorite terms are "cold" and "free."

gyle—A quantity of beer brewed at one time; a brewing. Each keg has a gyle number to indicate its brewing. We've got a huge gyle collection.

jirble—To pour a drink unsteadily. After a few rounds of Dunk the Duchess, players always jirble.

zymurgy—The branch of chemistry dealing with fermentation, distillation, and wine-making. Really, the only good reason to be a science major.

With thanks to Paul Dickson's book **Words** *(Delacorte Press, 1982).*

BOOT FACTOR TWO

The Boot Factor Two games teach fundamental principles of beer gaming while still boasting a low regurgitation potential. With these contests, the gamester can acquire and hone the skills that earn survival in most upper-level games: mastering the unique verbal and non-verbal language associated with beer gaming, knowing whom *not* to sit next to (lightweights are always the first to york), and training your bladder to retain many more ounces of fluid than it has ever held before.

Chug Boat	Beer Softball
Hi, Bob	Categories
Thumper	Pookie
Famous Names	Fuzzy Duck
Tang	Beergammon
Beer Shooting	Beer Checkers
Boat Racing	

Chug Boat

Boot Factor: 2

Did you ever wonder how Doc on *Love Boat* managed to score so often with the babes? So did we, but it doesn't have anything to do with **Chug Boat.**

Now, we know that no one would really *plan* to watch *Love Boat*, right? But just in case you turn it on by accident and start

getting hypnotized by the idiotic plot, at least you can do the sensible thing and crack open a few brewskis. The show often airs mid-morning, so this can be a great way to start the day.

Playing **Chug Boat** is as easy as some of the guest stars on the show. Each player chooses a "regular" (the Captain, Doc, Gofer, Julie, Vicki, or Isaac), and the player drinks whenever his character appears on the screen. The boat itself is also a viable character, and players who choose the *Pacific Princess* must drink each time there's a full-length shot of the boat. If the main plot revolves around your character, you'll begin to think you really *are* on some kind of cruise.

There's only one more rule: whenever there's a gratuitous shot of a well-endowed female sauntering across the deck in a revealing outfit, everyone must yell "Balloon smugglers!" and drink.

If you play **Chug Boat** during a two-hour special, the game is more appropriately called "Love Boot."

(**Note:** Similar rules can be applied to most every long-running TV show. Contributors to the Beer Research Dept. [see pg. 144] have sent games for *Star Trek, Cheers, Friends, Bay Watch*, and so on. Like we needed another reason to watch *Bay Watch*.)

Hi, Bob

Boot Factor: 2

For couch potatoes who are not satisfied with just **Chug Boat**, there's **Hi, Bob**, played while watching *The Bob Newhart Show*. The only rules are that everyone must drink half a glass of beer whenever a character says, "Bob," and chug a full glass when a character says, "Hi, Bob."

Sound easy? Guess again. You'll be amazed how television screenwriters create scripts with drinking games in mind.

Nine Foreign Terms for "Hangover"

1. *katzenjammer* (German for "the wailing of cats")
2. *stonato* (Italian for "out of tune")
3. *la gueule de bois* (French for "wooden throat")
4. *resaca* (Spanish for "surf of the sea")
5. *jeg har tommermen* (Norwegian for "carpenters in my head")
6. *hont i haret* (Swedish for "pain in the roots of my hair")
7. *ire Rasta coco ganja* (Jamaican for "stoned Rastafarian trying to split my coconut")
8. *so to gi ko-ho!* (Vietnamese for "water buffalo plowing inside my head")
9. *byt v druhom stave* (Slovak for "to be in a second state")

Thumper

Boot Factor: 2

Thumper is essentially a tag game with sign language. Each player chooses a simple sign that he can make with one or two hands: tugging the ear, thumbs up, O.K., choking on a half-chewed piece of steak, etc.

To begin, players sit in a circle and start thumping in a rhythmic fashion, slapping both hands twice against their thighs or the table, then clapping their hands twice, and repeating. The player starting the round says, "What's the name of the game?" and all the players answer, "Thumper!" Then he asks, "How do you play?" and they answer, "Signs!" He then makes his own sign during the two slapping beats and then the sign of another player on the clapping beats. Whoever's sign was just introduced must make his own sign during the next slapping beats and then the sign of yet another player on the claps.

The difficulty lies in tying this together: recognizing your sign, remembering the sign of another player, and maintaining the beat. At all times, anyone not signing must be thumping. Players drink when they are incapable of signing to the beat or when they make the sign of the player who has just made their sign. A fast beat can make **Thumper** a uniquely devastating game.

Thumper is well-suited for boy/girl or fraternity/sorority contests, especially when risqué signs are used. If the right signals are sent, who knows? Perhaps a little one-on-one **Thumper** may follow...

Famous Names

Boot Factor: 2

The next time someone accuses you, a dedicated and knowledgeable beer gamester, of being ignorant about current events, grab your drinking buddies, tap a keg, and challenge this bonehead to play **Famous Names**. He will soon discover that beer drinkers can be exceedingly well-informed people.

One player starts the game by saying the first and last name of a "famous" person—that is, a well-known living, dead, or fictitious character. The next player must name a famous person whose first name begins with the first letter of the previous famous person's last name. Got it? The game continues around the circle in this way, and the doofus who can't think of a new name in a few seconds must drink and start the new round.

For example, a fairly impressive round might go like this: Thurston Howell, Herman Munster, Marcia Brady, Beaver Cleaver, Charles Bronson, Barney Rubble, Rickie Lee Jones, John Kennedy, k.d. lang, L.L. Bean, Bruce Springsteen, Shaquille O'Neal, and so on.

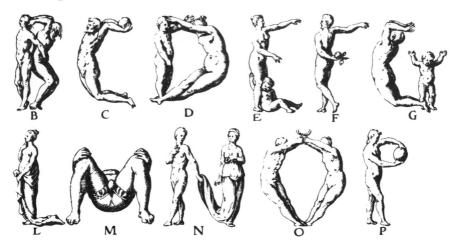

To increase the challenge, add two rules. If both names of the famous person begin with the same letter (Ronald Reagan, Howard Hughes, Moses Malone), the order of play is instantly reversed. Ditto if the famous person has only one name (Cher, Madonna, Moses).

Hook the beer-gaming skeptic on **Famous Names**, and it should be no problem to lure him into **Quarters**, **Boot-a-Bout**, and other, more meaningful, pursuits. And any parent, employer, or professor certainly will be impressed by this demonstration of your knowledge of the world around you. At the very least, it proves you can read *People* magazine.

*(**Hint**: The names Johnny Quest, Malcolm X, and Pia Zadora are almost sure winners.)*

" The government that increases the price for beer necessarily falls."
Jaroslav Hasek, Czech writer

Tang

Boot Factor: 2

Invented by Yale students in the 1940's, **Tang** is a venerable team drinking sport, and it has nothing to do with the space-age, orange-like juice of the same name. To spectators, the game looks like just another chugging match, but its many technical and strategic nuances make it something much more. At Yale, teams practice for the entire school year before going head-to-head in a wet, beer-inhaling showdown.

Two teams of ten must line up on opposite sides of a long table. In front of each player rest two eight-ounce glasses of beer filled to the brim. Each player assumes the Tanging position beneath the table. A referee dips his thumb up to the first knuckle into each glass to assure that all are equally full. (As the referee submerges his thumb, beer should flow freely over the rim of the glass. If not, he adds more beer and re-tests the glass.)

After checking all the glasses and asking the players if they are ready, the referee announces, "Practice taps" and raps an empty bottle on the table three times slowly and rhythmically. He then says, "Real thing" and taps three times again at the same pace. On the third tap, two timekeepers click their stopwatches, and the first drinker on each team chugs his first glass of beer. When the glass is empty, the player must slam it down on the table, thus signaling to the next team member to chug his first glass. When the second player slams his glass, the third chugs, and so on down the line.

As the glasses pound down along the table, the race will approach the tenth player, known as the "corner man." This player should be the swiftest drinker on the team, because he must down *both* his beers, one after the other. After the corner man finishes his second beer, the race reverses direction and goes back up the line—player #9 must drink his second beer, then #8, and so on.

When the first players from each team—the guys who started it all in the first place—slam down their glasses, the timekeepers stop their watches and note the elapsed time. Before

A Tang match at Yale. Can you spot Scott in the crowd?

the referee can announce the true victor, he must check each drinker for infractions and assess any penalties, and this is where the quality of the drinking becomes a factor. If the drinker has spilled, snarfed, or left in his glass more than a tablespoon of beer, the referee declares him a "gross wet" and adds three penalty seconds onto his team's time. If the drinker has left or spilled less than a tablespoon, he is declared a "wet," and the referee penalizes his team 1.5 seconds. But if the player drank everything and spilled nothing, the referee calls "clean drink" and assesses no penalty.

Hence, a speedy chugger averaging one second per beer can ruin his superb time with just one gross wet—and thus sink his team. A moderately paced, clean-drinking team will almost always beat a fast, wet one. (There's probably a Grand Moral Conclusion from this, but we don't know what it is.)

Though veteran Tangers appear nonchalant as they swallow an eight-ounce brew in under a second, these quaffers have perfected their art through diligent practice and a shrewd use of certain tricks. Careful study of these athletes can greatly help the beginning Tanger. Here are some specific suggestions:

- Before the race, warm the beer to room temperature and de-carbonate it by shaking or stirring. Those chilly little bubbles can cause an embarrassing snarf.

- Wet the front of your shirt before you get to the table so that any spillage won't be so noticeable to the referee. This trick works especially well for co-ed teams.

- Position your body under the table, with your chin right on the edge, so you can throw your head all the way back. Keeping low gives the glass less distance to travel and saves crucial femtoseconds.

- Exhale immediately before you chug. Otherwise, your inflated lungs will constrict your esophagus.

Above all, relax. Nervousness tightens the throat and makes for an unsteady hand, the downfall of many a Tanger. You must establish an intimate relationship with your beer. Let yourself be one with the liquid before you, so that Tanging becomes a swift, natural act. Watching reruns of *Kung Fu* helps.

The "corner man" must tang his two beers consecutively.

Beer Shooting

Boot Factor: 2

Beer shooting is not really a drinking game. Rather, it's a style of drinking beer. Fast. It can also be a sign of machismo. Like the peacock's feathers, the deer's antlers, or the length of a guy's johnson, the ability to shoot a beer, to the informed, demonstrates virility.

Hold an unopened can of brew upside-down and puncture it with a can opener as near to the bottom of the can as possible. The "shooter" places his mouth over the hole and sucks as much air and beer into his mouth as he can, creating a vacuum in the can—visible as it dents inward. He then turns the can right side up, still sucking on the hole, and pops open the top. The beer will explode into the player's mouth, sometimes faster than he can swallow.

The combination of the cold, high-velocity beer stream and the stinging carbonation overwhelms most beginners. It is only the seasoned "shooter" who can inhale a beer properly without drooling or snarfing. Smashing the spent can against the side of your head, then emitting a sonic belch, completes this display of supreme studliness.

Boat Racing

Boot Factor: 2

In essence, **Boat Racing** is the British version of **Tang**. Since the game requires only players and beer—the lowest common denominator of beer gaming—it's a perfect drinking game for a bar. **Boat Racing** is especially suited for the crew jocks in the crowd.

Each team of nine people lines up in the fashion of a crew in its shell. That is, eight players stand in a single file line, and the smallest (or lightest) member of the team—known as the "coxswain" or "cox"—stands at the front of the line, facing the others.

Each member of the "boat" has a full mug of brew, and the race begins with the coxswain, who chugs his beer as fast as he can. When he's finished, he places his glass upside-down on his head, thus signaling the next player in line (the first person facing the cox) to chug. When this player is finished, he too inverts his glass on his head, and the player behind him starts to chug, and so on down the line. The team that reaches the end of its "boat" first is the winner. (Remember, it's the duty of the cox to pace his team by shouting, "Stroke! Stroke!" and to encourage them by yelling, "Power chug!" at crucial moments.)

Inverting your cup on your head assures everyone that you have indeed finished your beer. For us Americans, a few drops of brew on the scalp hardly seems a severe penalty. (Indeed, it can leave your hair lustrous and full of body.) But remember, this is a British game, and our friends from the lapsed empire are a tad on the daintier side.

Those who are especially outrageous and/or devious will realize that it is quite legal for each player to simply pour his beer on his head without bothering to drink any of it. Though we consider this waste sinful, you can beat the other "boats" by a mile with this method. This trick works once, maybe twice, a night.

A coxswain and his crew.

After real crew races, it's customary for the members of the losing boat to give their shirts to their victorious opponents. It's a fine tradition to uphold if you're playing against the Playboy Centerfolds' Drinking Team, but if you're just playing against the usual slobs at the pub, don't bother. The losers at least should buy the winners the next round, though.

Played often enough, **Boat Racing** is affectionately known as — you guessed it — "Boot Racing."

"Beer and skittles ... form a good part of every Englishman's education."
Thomas Hughes, *Tom Brown's Schooldays*

Beer Softball

Boot Factor: 2

Softball is an honored part of our national heritage, but let's face it: the game is just an elaborate beer-delivery apparatus. In the spirit of the Constitution, **Beer Softball** introduces a system of checks and balances to the typical game: the more you get on base, the more you drink. Athletic superiority is thereby held in check by increasing amounts of brew.

Since **Beer Softball** has been around so long, there are many variations. The classic version requires that all base-runners consume some portion of a beer, usually half a cup, before passing any base.

There are several difficulties with this. First, making sure all those beers are ready for consumption at each base can be a logistical nightmare. Players are wise to appoint a Beer Bimbo—usually someone's little brother or sister—who will faithfully serve the bases. Second, the game can proceed quite slowly, especially when timid drinkers find their way into the festivities. Third, after a few home runs from the hot batters, you'll need replacements for these wounded sluggers. Babe Ruth would have been a lot pudgier if he had played in this league.

Our favorite version of **Beer Softball** is a little more convenient (and survivable). Place a keg behind second base. All base-runners must finish a whole cup of beer before passing, and the second baseman and the shortstop make sure that there are always plenty of cups filled.

Categories

Boot Factor: 2

Categories is perfect if you want to play a quick beer game between classes or during a coffee break at work.

Someone starts by naming a "category," which can be most anything—brands of European beer, Oscar winners, hot freshmen, whatever. One by one, players must name something in that category. The first person who fails to offer an original addition to the category in a reasonable time must drink.

The game is great for trivia buffs. You might consider passing on a round if your opponent comes up with categories like "Uruguayan Rock Stars" or "Scenic Spots in New Jersey."

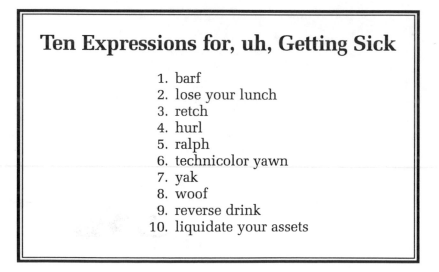

Ten Expressions for, uh, Getting Sick

1. barf
2. lose your lunch
3. retch
4. hurl
5. ralph
6. technicolor yawn
7. yak
8. woof
9. reverse drink
10. liquidate your assets

Pookie

Boot Factor: 2

One of the world's most underrated spectator sports is **Pookie**. To play, a beer gamer stands about six inches from a wall, tosses either a golf ball or a Ping-Pong ball into the air close to the wall, and tries to pin it to the wall with his forehead. If a player misses, he will smash his face into the wall. Fun, right?

Obviously, **Pookie** was developed for the low-forehead football crowd, but even the perfect preppie profile can be an advantage. Indeed, an upturned prep nose is well-suited for the most demanding maneuver in **Pookie**—the Nose Ball. This feat requires the player to throw the ball up and, instead of pinning it, to flip it up again with his nose. He then pins it with his forehead in the usual manner.

The rules for **Pookie** resemble those for **Quarters**. A player successfully pinning the ball decides who must drink and then goes again. A successful Nose Ball forces everyone to chug.

Players may risk a "double"—if they don't pin their first throw, they can toss again. If they miss a second time, they must drink, and the next player throws.

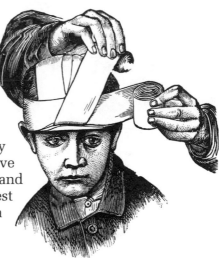

A few words on strategy: do not play while wearing glasses, do not play with an open head wound, do not play against brick walls, and do not play sober. Golf balls hurt and leave red welts on your forehead and face. Ping-Pong balls are best but can collapse during a pin, resulting in a penalty drink for destroying equipment. And only wussies play with Nerf balls.

Another happy Pookie player

The combination of a migraine and a hangover, characteristic of the morning after a **Pookie** tournament, is unique. If it lasts more than a week, or if you have the urge to play again, see a doctor. You need your head examined.

**"And malt does more than Milton can
To justify God's ways to man.
Ale, man, ale's the stuff to drink
For fellows whom it hurts to think."
A.E. Housman, *A Shropshire Lad***

Twenty Ways to Say "Drink"

1. pound	11. flush
2. quaff	12. drain
3. suck	13. swig
4. shoot	14. inhale
5. polish off	15. chow bev
6. do a 12-ounce curl	16. tipple
7. imbibe	17. nurse
8. potate	18. toss
9. guzzle	19. gulp
10. chug	20. bend the elbow

Fuzzy Duck

Boot Factor: 2

Fuzzy Duck is a game of oral dexterity. Even fast-talking, pre-law types will have a tough time with this one.

To play, participants assemble in a circle, and the first player begins this verbal tag game by looking at the person on his right and saying, "Fuzzy duck." This second player now looks to his right and also says, "Fuzzy duck." This continues around the circle until someone decides to reverse the direction of the game. To do this, a player must look at the person who just gave him the "fuzzy duck" (on his left) and ask, "Duzzy?" This not only sends the game in the opposite direction but also changes the passing words from "fuzzy duck" to "ducky fuzz."

The game continues in this new direction, with each player looking to his left and saying, "Ducky fuzz" until another player asks, "Duzzy?", reversing the direction again and changing the passing words back to "fuzzy duck." The turkey who gets tongue-tied or breaks the tempo must drink and start the new round.

Even fledglings will realize that "fuzzy duck" and "ducky fuzz" can be twisted into hilarious, obscene phrases, making **Fuzzy Duck** especially fun to play with unsuspecting parents, priests, or professors.

Beergammon

Boot Factor: 2

Though few would disagree that backgammon is one of the best games ever invented, even fewer realize that it can be greatly improved with a simple addition: beer. No, even humanity's oldest board game isn't sacred.

To play **Beergammon,** play a normal game of backgammon using the doubling cube. When the game is over, the loser must drink one-fourth of a beer for every point lost.

For example, if the game was a double game, the loser drinks half a beer. No problem. But if the game was 8, 16, or 32 points, the consequences can be frightening. Lose a 64-point game, and you're toast.

To add another twist, you can play **Beergammon** so that every time a player's piece is hit and sent to the bar, he must chug half a beer. Thus, not only is a defeated player penalized for losing the game, he also suffers *during* the game as well. To make matters worse, some **Beergammon** fans play for up to $1.00 a point, on top of the suds. That way, you can lose your shirt as well as your lunch.

Ten More Expressions for Getting Sick

1. negative chug
2. scream at the bushes
3. laugh at the carpet
4. shout at your shoes
5. regurgitate
6. blow doughnuts
7. blow groceries
8. blow chow
9. blow chunks
10. blow lunch

Beer Checkers

Boot Factor: 2

Beer Checkers is not meant for old men on park benches. Rather, mixing beer and checkers makes the most boring game on earth really come to life.

To play, merely substitute Dixie cups or shot glasses filled with beer for the checkers. When your cup is jumped, you drink it. And when your pieces make it across the board, instead of "kinging" them and making them double shots, you can replace the beer with a shot of hard booze.

Opposing players should use different colors or styles of shot glasses. Or, better yet, use light and dark beer.

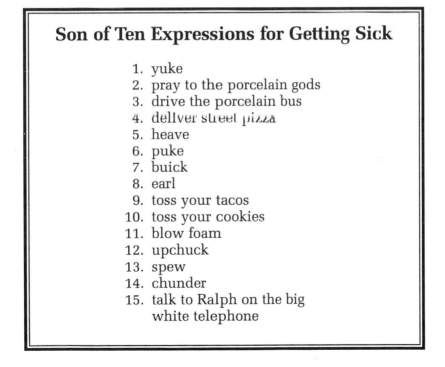

Son of Ten Expressions for Getting Sick

1. yuke
2. pray to the porcelain gods
3. drive the porcelain bus
4. deliver street pizza
5. heave
6. puke
7. buick
8. earl
9. toss your tacos
10. toss your cookies
11. blow foam
12. upchuck
13. spew
14. chunder
15. talk to Ralph on the big white telephone

Twenty Characteristics of a Truly Classic Bar

1. Good jukebox (rock, Motown, Sinatra, no rap)
2. Cheap pitchers
3. Walls cluttered with collegiate memorabilia
4. Bathroom with no locks, no toilet paper, no mirror, and good graffiti
5. No waitresses or service of any kind
6. Munchies available (especially hard-boiled eggs, beer nuts, and pretzels)
7. Wood tables carved with lots of initials
8. Real, old-fashioned pinball machines, coin-operated pool table, shuffleboard, etc.
9. Absence of hanging plants
10. Bushes outside for convenient late-night watering
11. Pizza readily available nearby
12. Six-foot TV screen (optional)
13. Greasy fries and burgers served all night
14. Equally greasy bartenders
15. Pay telephone available to wake up wimp roommates
16. Lots of happy hours and beer specials
17. Broken neon sign
18. Menthol odor from sanitary pucks (a.k.a. urinal candy) vaguely noticeable throughout establishment
19. Big wood booths without cushions
20. Year-round Christmas decorations

BEER FINISHING SCHOOL

Or, Some Cool Party Tricks

No matter how hard they try, beer drinkers will never be accepted by their peers until they are well-versed in the drinking graces. Naturally, they must know their beer and their beer games, but that's not enough. Refining certain drinking skills—from silly tricks to impressive displays of drinking prowess—is simply *de rigueur*. This knowledge distinguishes the cultured imbiber from the crude swiller.

Can crushing is a skill that provides a laugh as well as a fine chance to display *machismo*. Dent the side of an empty aluminum beer can slightly, place it against your head, and squash into your skull. This stunt was made famous by the late John Belushi in the film classic, *Animal House*.

❖

Bottle Cap Flipping: By hooking a bottle cap over your thumb and snapping your middle finger across it, you can turn a cap into a deadly, Frisbee-like projectile. The virtuoso is ambidextrous and can flip caps behind his back, between his legs, and over his head in rapid succession.

❖

The **beer sneeze**, a great party trick, is sure to draw a chuckle or a punch in the nose. Sneak up behind your target and place an unopened can very close to his exposed neck. When you pop the top, loudly fake a sneeze at the same time. The object of the prank will think you've sneezed all over his neck. The advanced sneezer can escape the scene without detection.

Sadly, **can biting** is on the verge of extinction. Yet, there is no other skill that better suggests the intimate relationship between drinker and beer. The drinker shakes an aluminum can and then bites into its side and drinks the beer as it sprays out wildly. He then tears the empty can to pieces with his teeth, while making the appropriate "Wild Kingdom" noises.

❖

Opening bottles with your teeth is an awe-inspiring skill that woos chicks and humbles guys. It's also practical at beach parties or on camping trips when a real bottle opener is nonexistent. This useful ability will earn you instant notoriety, as well as an outrageous orthodontist's bill.

❖

Reverse-handed drinking is a technique that appears difficult but is actually a piece of cake. Before you pick up your beer, rotate your hand 180-degrees towards you, then grab the brew and drink. Friends will envy your drinking dexterity. Note: If you rotate *after* grabbing the beer, you will look really spastic.

❖

Ear drinking is a sleight-of-hand that leaves drunk spectators baffled. Use a half-filled beer to fake pouring liquid into your ear, while simultaneously letting beer secretly held in your mouth drain into a cup. For most, such a feat is just a clever trick. But for those named "Lumpy," "Moose," or "Brandee," it may actually be possible.

❖

Nose drinking has its greatest effect when you are wearing a coat and tie and having a serious conversation about investments, politics, or other such mature stuff. Nonchalantly hoist a beer to your nose, tilt your head back, and swallow. Continue your conversation as if you had just done the most natural thing in the world.

❖

Waterfall pouring looks impressive and is a way to drink without stopping to change or refill cups. Start drinking from a cup, and pour beer into it as you drink. For even more fun, let friends join in and pour their beer into your cup, too. You may never have to pay for beer again!

❖

Bottle bombing is a great outlet for many frustrations. Fill a beer bottle (long-necks are preferable) with water about an inch below the top and, while holding the neck, vigorously strike the mouth of the bottle with the flat of your other palm. The bottle's bottom half will explode off with a satisfying "whommmmpft" and a crash of glass. Extremely cool.

❖

Draäling beer, the finishing touch for the truly skilled drinker, is a Norwegian practice in which the drinker places a bottle of beer to his lips and swings it in a circular motion. This elephantine maneuver causes the beer to swirl inside the bottle and shoot out rapidly without glugging as the drinker tilts his head back.

❖

Pouring beer on your head requires little dextcrity and even less intelligence. It is, however, good for a laugh and a great thing to do just before passing out. In addition, this commendable practice leaves your hair shiny, clean, and manageable.

Our friend Drew has beautiful hair.

The Road Trip

Road trip. *It's a phrase that evokes images of mystery, adventure, camaraderie, and eager women. And anything with all this great stuff is naturally a rite of passage for most red-blooded college males.*

Those who have never road-tripped may wonder what all the fuss is about. Well, we invite all novices to travel with us as we recount our last great voyage and prove that a road trip is essential to the college experience.

———◆●◆———

It was a really boring night on campus. The only activities were a wine and cheese reception at the art gallery, a sing-along jamboree, and a recent Woody Allen movie. Clearly, anyone who had ever produced a single ounce of testosterone would not be seen within a hundred yards of these events. There was only one option: *Road Trip*!

Naturally, we were exicted about the possibilities that lay ahead—*heh, heh, heh*—but we had to make a few plans. The first task was to draw straws to see who would drive. This is perhaps the most tense moment of the journey, since the poor driver is forbidden to touch one drop of alcohol. Thus, he must endure his comrades' hijinks, which are always less than hysterical to someone who's sober.

Our next chore: find the proper vehicle. The dirtier and more beat-up the car, the better suited to the spirit of the trip. But there's also a practical reason for getting a bomb: if you take a nice car, it's not likely to return that way. The car must also be hopelessly undersized for the number of occupants. As a general rule, compacts hold 8-10 people, and station wagons

Andy uses his patented Beernoculars™ to find free brew.

15-20. We had about 10 guys, so we got a shoddy compact.

Before leaving, most of us took brief power naps to ensure we'd have the extra energy we'd nood later to concoct brilliant lines like, "So, what's your major?"

After the naps, we got motivated and wedged ourselves into the car. Even though we weren't planning to return until the next morning, no one was permitted to bring any luggage. Baggage would only ruin the spontaneity of the adventure. Except toothbrushes. Those are okay.

The first stop was a package store, where we bought a few cases of roadies for the passengers. Also known as *road pops, road sauce,* and *tweeners,* roadies are key to any road trip. Mainly, they serve to inflate the road tripper's ego to staggering proportions. We had to believe that, upon our arrival, we would each command the undying attention of at least 15 women. The roadies also encourage the ritualistic pit stop at the side of the highway. After all, you never buy beer, you only rent it. (Scenic overlooks are highly recommended.)

This pit stop is the only break allowed on a true road trip; the car is not even permitted to slow down to dispense the empties. For this task, experienced road trippers appoint a "bombardier"—usually the person located next to a window or under the sun roof—who is charged with tossing empties at road signs, obnoxious dogs, and various rock formations.

Well-provisioned, we went rocketing into the night like an unguided libido. About 10 miles down the road, we realized that we hadn't decided where we were going. Actually, this wasn't too important, since many road trippers don't know where they are when they get there. All they know is they've finished their roadies, and they must seek the nearest keg party, any keg party. And women, any women.

At last, after an hour or so, we arrived at our Valhalla, the land of beer and honeys: a sorority mixer at Mt. Smith-Hollins College. We attacked the kegs and scoped the scene. Not great, but definitely some talent. We started to mingle among the crowd—a little chit-chat here, a little dancing there—to see if any women wanted to "buy some tickets to Boomtown." Not much response. We are told that guys like us are "only interested in one thing." So? Explaining that it was our biological imperative didn't seem to help much, either.

After a few hours of cuddling the keg a little and striking out a lot, we decided it was a lost cause and we should rally the troops and head for home. Unfortunately, our driver had disappeared. It seems that he was the only one sober enough to get a girl to talk to him, so he was nowhere in sight.

Undaunted, we settled on nearby couches and under convenient pianos and began concocting orgiastic stories to tell our lightweight roommates who stayed behind. After all, they missed an awesome road trip.

"Drink! for you know not whence you came, nor why; Drink! for you know not why you go, nor where."
The Rubbaiyat of Omar Khayyám

BOOT FACTOR THREE

Penalties in **Boot Factor Three** games are generally no more stringent than those in Boot Factor Two. However, since they require more mental and physical agility, Boot Factor Three games are more difficult to play. At this level, players tend to falter more often and therefore drink more frequently. But violent heaves are still uncommon, although players will sometimes opt for the self-induced ralph (a.k.a. "bootlimia") to mollify the next morning's hangover.

Beer Golf	I Never
Whales Tails	Mexican
Swim Relays	Cardinal Puff
Bullshit	Quarters
Frisbeer	Fizz Buzz
Cups	Zoom, Schwartz,
Dunk the Duchess	Perfigliano

Beer Golf

Boot Factor: 3

Some people play golf sober. Really!
We don't. Ever. Neither should you.

Beer Golf differs from sober golf in one respect: linksters may deduct one stroke for every beer they consume during a round. (A round usually consists of only nine holes—even Jack and Arnie would have problems with eighteen.) No other handicaps are permitted.

Most beer golfers swig a frostie per hole and then chug several on the final fairway. Those choosing a more ambitious pace discover the Principle of Diminishing Returns. Many also discover the meaning of octuple bogey.

Beer Golf is usually played in the form of a fraternity or club outing, which brings to light two of the game's disadvantages. First, participants must actually plan ahead, a concept completely alien to most beer game ideology. Second, players can never try **Beer Golf** twice at the same course—with the management's permission, that is. Greenskeepers are rarely amused at golf carts sunk in water hazards, 9-irons used as putters, or fairways littered with empties.

"One more drink and I'll be under the host."
Dorothy Parker

Whales Tails

Boot Factor: 3

Whales Tails may very well make *you* an endangered species. This fast-paced game will challenge anyone's ability to stay afloat.

Basically a verbal form of "Tag, you're it," **Whales Tails** requires six or more players sitting in a circle. To play, one person begins by chanting, "Whales Tails, Prince of Wales, Prince in the Court of (*number*) calls (*number*)." The first number is the total number of players, including the speaker. The second number designates a player that many places to the *left* of the speaker.

So, if the speaker calls "five," he's calling on the player five places to his left around the circle. This person becomes the Prince and responds, "Nay," and the speaker then asks, "Who?" The Prince responds by calling another number, which represents the number of places to his left that "it" is passed.

The game continues in this way until someone makes a mistake or breaks the tempo. When this happens, the person responsible must drink. This game is much harder than you might think, because each player's distance from the Prince changes every few moments as new Princes ascend the throne.

To increase the game's difficulty, the speaker may call a number higher than the total number playing. Thus, if there are 10 players and the Prince calls "13," then "it" goes once around the circle and ends up three places to the speaker's left. The speaker may also call his own number (equal to the number of people playing), which allows him to go again.

If everyone begins to catch on, switch places every few rounds. Better yet, introduce "reversals" to the game. For instance, whenever the Prince calls a multiple of five, the game travels in the opposite direction. Such permutations— in a game that already requires far too much thought and attention for beer-sodden players—is guaranteed to get everyone harpooned.

Fifteen Ways to Say "Drunk"

1. soused
2. plastered
3. corked
4. lit-up
5. scuppered
6. bent out of shape
7. faced
8. squashed
9. trashed
10. wiped-out
11. plowed
12. swamped
13. blasted
14. reeling
15. muddled

Swim Relays

Boot Factor: 3

Swim Relays, like geese, can be found only in Florida during the winter. To participate, you must head south, say to Daytona Beach during Spring Break.

Swim Relays are staged at bars or hotels that have pools and are usually held before the wet t-shirt contest (which is what people have really come to see, of course). Teams are formed along college or fraternity lines. At the gun, the first swimmer for each team chugs a beer and then swims the length of the pool. The second swimmer then chugs his beer and swims back, and so on until one team wins.

We discourage you from trying this at home unless your pool has a very good filtration system. The "aqua boot" is not a pretty sight.

Bullshit

Boot Factor: 3

Bullshit is one of the many beer games that expand the realm of human knowledge, focusing on oft-overlooked aspects of animal physiology. **Bullshit** needs no accessories, so you can play easily anywhere or any time. But considering its ribald content, we suggest you avoid playing at the ballet, at funerals, and in court.

The game begins with the Master of Ceremonies asking players what brand of animal, uh, feces they wish to be. For instance, a player can choose horseshit, dogshit, batshit, shrimpshit, wormshit, or even squidshit. The emcee initiates the round by saying, "Somebody shit in the parlor." All players respond in unison, "Who shit?" The emcee blames one of the players: "Dogshit," for example. Being accused, Dogshit must reply, "Bullshit!" (as in, "Bullshit! I did not!"). The emcee asks, "Who shit?" and Dogshit responds with one of the other names; say, "Catshit." Thus the game continues, with Catshit saying, "Bullshit!" and Dogshit responding, "Who shit?" and Catshit blaming someone else.

This goes on until someone breaks the rhythm or responds out of turn or incorrectly. Then, naturally, the shit-for-brains drinks. This drinker is the new Master of Ceremonies and must initiate the next round.

Here are some of the more interesting types of shit that we have encountered during our research: Barney, mahimahi, velociraptor, eel, Beavis, Terminator, tapeworm, Cindy Brady, iguana, Flipper, aardvark, pterodactyl, guppy, amoeba, Mr. Ed, Bambi, tsetse fly, and Clinton.

Of course, any type of shit that pops out is just fine. You should note that two killer shits are "eweshit" (sounds like "you shit" or "who shit") and "bullshit." Both are legal and make the game even more confusing.

After you've played a number of rounds and everyone has become accustomed to the assigned names, it's time to change identities. Better yet, change the names before they become too familiar. This keeps people on their toes and drinking. It's also legal to introduce non-animal "shits." For example, try the following: eatshit, softshit, I-shit, you-shit, he-shit, we-shit, and shitshit.

Fifteen More Ways to Say "Drunk"

1. boxed
2. wasted
3. basted
4. hammered
5. shellacked
6. stinko
7. blitzed
8. gassed
9. primed
10. skunked
11. slaughtered
12. stiff
13. gooned
14. gone Borneo
15. smashed

Frisbeer

Boot Factor: 3

In an effort to distribute more equitably the destruction of brain cells, we decided we needed a game to appeal to the mellow, grungy, "cooler-than-thou" types, as well as the fraternity/beach crowd. So, we invented **Frisbeer**, and we take full blame.

One summer day, we were lounging around the beach, casually tossing that apotheosized disk of plastic, the Frisbee (invented by Yalies of yore, incidentally). Agreeing that we were burning far too many calories with all the running around, we made an executive decision to bring beer into the picture. **Frisbeer** was born.

Frisbeer has little structure, so the kind of people who normally throw Frisbees a lot will take right to it. Two players start about 30 or 40 yards apart and place a bottle or can of beer in front of them. The players then take turns throwing a Frisbee at each other's beer. If your beer is hit, you must take a healthy gulp and walk one pace toward your opponent. This continues until the players are right on top of each other, making for some pretty rapid suds-sucking.

Once next to each other, players begin to pace in *opposite* directions until they are again about 30 or 40 yards apart. At this point, the players start to walk toward each other again. This process can continue, well, as long as you can walk.

If there are more than two players, participants should start by forming a geometric shape, with one competitor at each vertex (an equilateral triangle for three, a square for four, a dodecagon for twelve, etc.). Each player throws to his right. If a player's beer is hit, he takes a pace toward the player who just threw. Players will begin to spiral toward the center and then spiral outward again. Such configurations often prove astonishing and/or cosmic to those partaking in substances less legal than beer. Oh, wow.

"'Twas a woman who drove me to drink, and I never had the courtesy to thank her for it."

W.C. Fields

Return of Fifteen Ways to Say "Drunk"

1. loaded
2. looped
3. out of control
4. slozzled
5. ripped
6. toasted
7. skewered
8. juiced
9. blotto
10. bagged
11. tanked
12. pie-eyed
13. paralytic
14. sauced
15. sopped

Cups

Boot Factor: 3

Cups is perfect for frugal gamesters who don't want to invest in equipment. All you need are beer and plastic cups.

The object of **Cups** is to flip your cup in the air at least one full revolution so that it lands standing up on either end. If a player flips the cup and it lands right side up, the next player in rotation must finish a whole cup of beer. If the cup lands upside down, the next player must drink just half a beer. If the cup lands on its side, the "flipper" must take a healthy sip of his beer. And if the cup rolls off the table, the flipper must drink a whole beer. After each flip, regardless of the outcome, the cup is passed.

When a cup lands on one of its ends, the player who must drink can decide to reverse the direction of the game simply by saying so before he flips his cup. The game travels in the new direction until another player reverses. The beauty of this rule is that it allows for head-to-head battles between neighboring players.

This game was originally developed to familiarize beer drinkers with an important accessory, the cup. **Cups** was unknown in ancient times (i.e., before the invention of fast food), when players drank only from bottles and cans. The advent of the keg party spawned the **Cups** craze, which has been growing steadily since the 1950's.

An interesting variation of **Cups** is **Cans**, in which players flip a full can of beer until it lands upright. When that happens, the next player in rotation must open the well-shaken can *under his nose* and then drink it. If the can rolls off the table or lands on its side, the thrower must take penalty drinks.

Dunk the Duchess

Boot Factor: 3

Dunk the Duchess lets you play submarine commander—coolly, calmly calculating the best way to submerge your opponent. We learned **Dunk the Duchess** on a foray to an Irish dive bar on Manhattan's West Side. We had so much fun that we finished nine pitchers before the bartender decided it was time for us to leave.

To begin, players need two full pitchers and one glass per person, plus one extra glass. Float the extra glass in one of the pitchers. The lip of the glass should protrude about an inch or so above the surface of the beer. (Depending on the type of glass used, you might need to pour a little beer into the glass to steady it.) A narrow, Pilsner-style glass that tapers toward the bottom has the best buoyancy.

Players then fill their glasses from the second pitcher and take turns pouring beer into the floating glass. Each player is responsible for the glass for five seconds (counted aloud) after he pours. After the five-count, the glass becomes the responsibility of the next player. Thus, the perfect pour is one that causes the glass to sink in six seconds, thereby screwing the next player before he even has time to pour. The player who sends the glass to the bottom of the pitcher must retrieve it—and relieve it of its new-found contents.

Near the end of a round, as the glass actually floats *below* surface level due to surface tension (science majors will immediately say, "Meniscus!" at this point), skillful drop-by-drop pours become crucial. It is illegal to steady your hand by resting the pouring cup on the edge of the pitcher.

Dunk the Duchess can be a blast and a great crowd-pleaser, but it gets very messy, and we recommend keeping several mung rags on hand.

I Never

Boot Factor: 3

I Never is a drinking version of the old games "20 Questions" and "Truth or Dare." Once you start playing, you may swear, "I never will play again."

One person starts the game by making an "I never" statement such as, "I never have been drunk," whether it's true or not. Each player who cannot truthfully agree with this statement must drink. (In this case, whoever *has* been drunk must drink.) If everyone playing can honestly agree with the "I never" just stated, then the player who offered the statement must drink.

Now, all this sounds pretty silly—until you imagine playing with a group of people who don't know each other very well. All you have to do is make some outlandish "I never" statement such as, "I never have had sex with anyone in this group" and then wait to see who drinks. The potential for abuse is unlimited.

Son of Fifteen Ways to Say "Drunk"

1. bombed
2. buzzed
3. pickled
4. gagged
5. soaked
6. brained
7. walloped
8. grogged
9. pissed
10. stoked
11. stained
12. twisted
13. shit-faced
14. wrecked
15. steamed

Mexican

Boot Factor: 3

In most beer games, a modicum of practice and skill can keep a player from drinking too much and blowing his groceries. But in **Mexican**, the gaming *hombre* is at the mercy of the dice. Whether he tosses his tacos and takes an unscheduled siesta depends little on his training for the game. A few unlucky rolls, a few unsuccessful bluffs, and the beer will mount faster than the Third World's debt.

The object of **Mexican** is to be the last player in the game. It begins with each player placing a die, known as the "scoring die," on the table in front of him, with the 6 showing. The first player shakes two "game dice" in a cup and turns the cup upside down on the table so that the roll is hidden. He peeks and re-covers the dice.

A roll of 1:2 is called a "Mexican" and is the best possible roll. The best other rolls, in decreasing value, are as follows: 6:6, 5:5, 4:4, 3:3, 2:2, 1:1, and then 6:5, 6:4, 6:3, 6:2, 6:1, 5:4, 5:3, 5:2, 5:1, 4:3, 4:2, 4:1, 3:2, 3:1.

After assessing his roll, the player turns to his left and either admits his roll or bluffs. The second player may then do one of two things:

1. He can choose to believe the first player's call. If he does, he must re-roll the game dice to try to beat the first player's roll.

2. He may accuse the first player of bluffing by saying, "You're bluffing," "No way, bud," "Eat me, hosehead," etc. The accused then must uncover his roll.

If the first player was indeed bluffing, the point goes to the challenger. Otherwise, the point goes to the accused.

In either case, the loser of a point receives a stiff penalty—generally half a cup or more—and must then turn his scoring die from 6 to 5. The game continues around the table, with the defeated player of each round consuming brew and then turning his scoring die down one.

When a player with a 1 showing on his scoring die loses a point, he must drink a larger than normal penalty and then leave the game. The game ends when only one player remains.

Hasta la vista, baby.

"Sometimes too much to drink is barely enough."

Mark Twain

Bride of Fifteen Ways to Say "Drunk"

1. polluted
2. gone
3. tight
4. slambasted
5. sloshed
6. cocked
7. canned
8. fired-up
9. jacked-up
10. fubar
11. tuned-out
12. faceless
13. potted
14. crocked
15. totaled

Cardinal Puff

Boot Factor: 3

Cardinal Puff is one of the oldest and best drinking games around. Unfortunately, we can't tell you the rules.

You see, the game's rules and traditions are maintained by a sacred order of members who call themselves "Cardinals." The only way to learn the game is to seek out a Cardinal— simply by asking everyone you meet, "Are you a Cardinal?"— and have him pass his knowledge on to you.

If you succeed in learning the game, which entails drinking every time you make a mistake while learning the ritual, then you become a Cardinal and a keeper of the game. The members of this secret, loyal society travel by the creed, "Once a Cardinal, always a Cardinal."

The original Cardinal Puff

Quarters

Boot Factor: 3

Without a doubt, **Quarters** is the most popular drinking game in America. The game's large and vocal following loves its portability and its exciting mix of chance, skill, revenge, and power drinking. Above all, the opportunity to make your opponent grovel at your feet simply because you can plunk a quarter into a cup of beer 10, 20, even 30 consecutive times gives boundless joy to sadistic gamesters.

The quintessential **Quarters** table is six-inch-thick Honduran mahogany smoothed to a glossy sheen with multiple coats of premium varnish. Of course, any bar table will suffice. The game begins with a beer-filled cup placed on the table in front of a player, who tries to bounce a quarter off the table so that it lands in the cup. If successful, the thrower gets to make any player drink all the beer in the cup. He may then throw again.

If the quarter hits the cup's rim, the thrower may re-toss. If he hits three rims in a row, however, he must drink the beer in the cup. When the thrower misses the cup completely, he can pass the cup to the next player, or he can call a "double." A "double" lets him throw again, but if he misses or hits the rim on the "double" throw, he drinks. If he sinks the quarter on a "double," he can make any opponent chug, but the thrower can't toss again, and he passes the cup and the quarter.

Suicide Quarters, a more intense version for real sickos, is played similarly, except a cup of beer is placed directly *behind* the first cup. If the quarter bounces too far and lands in the second cup, the thrower must drink *both* cups. All the other rules are the same as one-cup **Quarters**. A rim shot on the second cup also means a re-throw. If the thrower hits three rims in a row on either cup, he drinks only one cup.

Quarters can and should be practiced anywhere, anytime. Give up twiddling your thumbs, biting your nails, and spanking your monkey, and dedicate that precious time instead to

Americo Quarterlucci, the first beer game missionary, taught a primitive version of Quarters to savage fraternities in the New World.

bouncing your quarter. Try different tossing techniques to determine your métier. One method is to hit the edge of the quarter on the table. Another is to bounce the flat face off the surface. (Most prefer the latter, since it gives more control.) Throwing consistently is truly an art; the motion must become ingrained, second nature, even genetic.

Besides throwing a quarter, chugging a brew with a quarter resting on the bottom lends another element of challenge to the game. The beer is properly polished off only when the drinker holds the empty cup in one hand and displays the quarter clenched between his front teeth. (Those readers in Appalachia without front teeth may hold the quarter between their lips.) There is, however, a direct correlation between degree of inebriation and frequency of quarter-ingesting. Many a neophyte player has exclaimed after chugging, "Whaddya mean there was a quarter in this cup?!" The x-rays are a hoot.

Above all, Quarters is a game of attack and revenge, screw and be screwed. A player gloating over a string of 15 consecutive sinks deserves to be punished. Repeatedly.

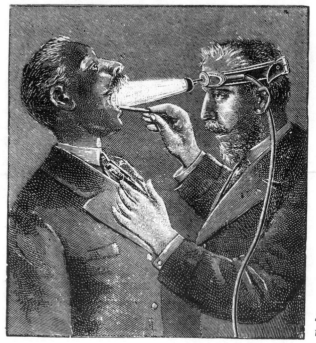

Searching for the quarter.

Fizz Buzz

Boot Factor: 3

If ever a game infuriated, infatuated, and intoxicated game-sters of all ages, **Fizz Buzz** is it. Though players need no math-ematical genius to succeed—we've played with math majors who hurled early and often—practiced regularly, **Fizz Buzz** should raise your standardized test scores at least ten percen-tile points.

Fizz Buzz is a counting game in which players try to reach higher levels of success on each round. The gist is this: when a player reaches a number that has a 5 in it (e.g., 5, 15, 25, 50, etc.) or is a multiple of 5 (10, 20, 30, etc.), he says "fizz" instead of the number. If a number has a 7 (7, 17, 27, 70, etc.) or is a multiple of 7 (7, 14, 21, etc.), he says "buzz" instead of the number. The apparent simplicity is deceiving.

One player starts by stating a number between 1 and 4 and saying "to my right" or "to my left" to indicate whether the player on his right or left continues. The next player then adds 1 to the number, and so on. The game continues in this way, with each player adding 1 and saying "fizz" or "buzz" when appropriate. Whenever anyone says "buzz," however, the direction of the game *reverses*.

Players will eventually realize that some numbers are mul-tiples of both 5 and 7 and/or include both 5 and 7, or two 5's or two 7's, for that matter. A number can get only one of the following designations: "fizz," "buzz," "fizz buzz," "fizz fizz," or "buzz buzz." We've already covered "fizz" and "buzz." The numbers that get "fizz buzz" are 35, 57, and 75 because they are multiples of 5 and 7 and/or include 5 and 7. The numbers that get "fizz fizz" are 15, 25, 45, 55, 65, etc. because they are multiples of 5 and include a 5. The only number worthy of the awesome, double-directional-changing "buzz buzz" is 77, a multiple of, and including, 7.

In our zeal to recount the game, we almost forgot to say that the player who breaks the game's tempo or says "bizz" or "fuzz" or "Damn, what number is it again?" must imbibe heavily and start the game all over.

As the game proceeds into the night, the practice and confidence of constant repetition is quickly offset by even small amounts of alcohol. A group that reached 40 or 50 at the start of an evening will be lucky to break 15 by the end.

A necessarily stern instructor at the Fizz Buzz Institute.

Zoom, Schwartz, Perfigliano

Boot Factor: 3

Zoom, Schwartz, Perfigliano, the word contest of choice for novices and experts alike, is a verbal tag game whose rules are easy to understand in theory—but nearly impossible to apply in practice.

One player begins by stating these exact words: "The name of the game is 'Zoom, Schwartz, Perfigliano'." At this point, the speaker is "it." The point is to keep passing "it" to other players without blundering.

At first, the only three commands are Zoom, Schwartz, and Perfigliano. To start, the speaker looks at another player and says, "Zoom." The player at whom the speaker was looking is now "it" and has three options:

1. He can look at any player except the person who just gave "it" to him and say, "Zoom." That player now is "it" and continues the game. You cannot "zoom" the person who just gave "it" to you.

2. He can look right back at the person who just gave "it" to him and say, "Schwartz." This gives "it" back to this player.

3. He can look at any player except the person who just gave him "it" and say, "Perfigliano." This also gives "it" right back to the first player.

The game continues with each new "it" tagging someone else according to these rules. Of course, as the game's tempo increases, **Z.S.P.** becomes very confusing, and everyone gets pretty shellacked. Note that direct eye contact with the person to whom a player is speaking is crucial; roving eyes indicate unfamiliarity with the rules and earn a penalty drink. An improper introduction (words deleted, rearranged, or added) also begets a penalty. The loser drinks and restarts the game until he gets it right.

Once players master three-word **Z.S.P.**, introduce additional titles. They are usually added one at a time in the following order: *Butaman, Coleman, Smith, Uncle Toby?*, and *Morowitz*. When the players have decided to add a new name, they must include it in their introduction from then on. For example, "The name of the game is 'Zoom, Schwartz, Perfigliano, Butaman, Coleman'." The new additions do the following:

- *Butaman* gives "it" to the player on the immediate right of the speaker—regardless of whom the speaker is looking a at when he says, "Butaman."

- *Coleman* gives "it" to the player on the immediate left of whomever the speaker is looking at when he says, "Coleman."

- *Smith* gives "it" to whoever says, "Smith." In effect, a "Smith" does nothing, but it can be used to stall or bait the gullible.

- *Uncle Toby?* gives "it" to the player two places to the right of whomever the speaker is looking at when he says, "Uncle Toby?" However, before the new "it" can continue the game, the person at whom the speaker was looking when he said, "Uncle Toby?" must respond "yes" in a low, drawn, Lurch-like voice—"Yeeeeesss." This person then does nothing, and the player two places to his right continues the game.*

- *Morowitz* transfers "it" to the player who spoke two turns before the "Morowitz" was used. For advanced players only.

Of course, these commands may be included or deleted on a whim. And it is perfectly legal and quite humorous to invent new titles. As the night rolls on, add titles like *Bobbitt* and create all the requisite sound effects, like snipping.

For anyone familiar with Yale, "Uncle Toby" is an inside joke at the expense of a certain secret society not renowned for its sense of humor.

IΠΓЯODUCΓiOΠ ΓO THE BEEЯ CUЯЯiCULUM

For better or worse, beer has always been closely linked with higher education. It's hard to imagine a contemporary college campus on which beer is not an important accessory, whether it's being served at an alumni fund-raiser or smuggled into the student section at a football game.

But beer's role in the hallowed halls of academe is not and should not be so limited. Beer is central to "the human condition," and by studying beer we can come to a better understanding of, well, just about everything! To illustrate this, we have developed a full semester of college courses based on our favorite topic.

"They who drink beer will think beer."
Washington Irving

HiSTORY 124
Beer: The Catalyst of History

What serious historian could doubt that beer has been the single most important factor in the development of civilization?

It all began over 20,000 years ago with the invention of the wheel, which gave men the means to road-trip to women's caves and prehistoric package stores. Cool as this was, however, there was a problem: man had not yet invented beer. So for ages, human progress was stagnant. Man demonstrated the intellectual prowess of Butt-head and the aesthetic appeal of a stegosaur. Life was slow, and man was slower. The species was waiting for an evolutionary catalyst (you know, like that black monolith thing in *2001: A Space Odyssey*). It was waiting for beer.

Suddenly, about 5,000 years ago, the Sumerians, history's original party dudes, put an end to the Stone Age by brewing the earth's first grog. These great guys ruled the world single-handedly for centuries and drank lots of homemade beer.

Then, one dark and embarrassing day, the power of the Sumerians was usurped by a clever group of men who drank wine and wore dresses—namely, the Greeks and Romans. These effete cads suppressed beer drinking for a millenium. Soon, feudal wars erupted throughout Europe, as people, fed up with religious persecution and medieval Blue Laws, demanded their right to drink the golden nectar again.

Fortunately, these Dark Ages were eventually enlightened by the Renaissance and the rebirth of art, science, and beer drinking. Men began to realize that life did not have to be entirely wretched and that you could party-down once in a while without incurring the wrath of some bishop, God, or other ecclesiastical bigwig.

Then, late in the 1600's, a group of guys facetiously known as the "Puritans" decided that living on the Continent had

A Sumerian hieroglyphic shows the brewing techniques of history's original party monsters.

become too much like *Donohue*—everybody was discussing their feelings, and no one wanted to just go out and get crazy. Fed up with this oppression, the Puritans packed their toothbrushes one Friday night and decided to road-trip to the New World. Also, they had heard there were babes there.

We can safely assume that the Puritans played some outrageous beer games during their journey on the *Mayflower*. After all, the captain's log describes passengers spending hours bent over the ship's railing, heaving into the Atlantic.

Though they had planned to arrive in Virginia, the Puritans were forced to land in Massachusetts because they ran out of beer. As they searched desperately for a convenience store, our partying forefathers decreed that in the New World, no French would be spoken, no fern bars would be built, and beer would always be on tap. These were the humble beginnings of a truly awesome nation.

Three and a half centuries have gone by, and America has been drinking beer and kicking butt ever since. We're 11-and-1 in major wars! We've invented everything worthwhile, except maybe Chinese food. Cars, planes, light bulbs, pizza, bowling, hamburgers, the telephone, and Elvis impersonators—the rest of the world owes us in a big way. And we know that they all secretly envy our nutty, beer-guzzling culture.

All in all, it seems clear that the U.S.A. has re-established the historic link between beer and world leadership.

What about Russia? you ask. Are you kidding? They drink vodka, for God's sake. Bad vodka at that. You might as well do shots of Pine-Sol. Japan? They drink *sake*, and never mind how it tastes—have you ever seen how small a *sake* cup is? You could never impose a healthy penalty chug with one of those tiny things. And China? Well, the Chinese are on the right track, because they love beer. We ought to send the space shuttle over there, loaded with cases of Rolling Rock. They'd cease all that childish communism stuff in a second.

Alas, not everything is rosy in this land of red, white, and amber. California wines have become quite popular, and daiquiri-serving fern bars have polluted urban areas everywhere. And then there are those damn wine coolers—if they're not subversive, we don't know what is. Not since we peed in the Central Park reservoir has there been a bigger threat to the drinking public.

Should these trends continue, we Americans could lose the mental toughness that keeps us on top. Let's face it, during the Iraq-Kuwait crisis, President Bush surely pounded some brewskis the night before he told Saddam to get bent. He did not sip Chardonnay.

We study history because we Americans can learn valuable lessons from the past, and because it's usually required for graduation. The lesson here is clear: beer drinkers don't mess around when it comes to world affairs. They get right to the top, and they stay there. We've got to keep socking down those frosties if we're going to keep the world safe for democracy, freedom, and rockin' keg parties.

So rally, America, rally!

BIOLOGY 150:

The Anatomy of a Hangover

Since necessity is the mother of invention, beer swillers have concocted some of the most elaborate, most vile, and most effective ways of dealing with that post-pleasure demon, Mr. Hangover.

But before we discuss the cures, we should consider the causes of a hangover. Simply, if you drink beer quicker than your liver can remove beer's alcohol and natural impurities called "congeners" from your blood, excess alcohol and congeners are free to cruise around your body and wreak havoc.

You see, the liver is where the chemistry-nerd cells of the body gather. When alcohol reaches these pale, calculator-toting misfits, they begin chemistry experiments to destroy it. But competition in the liver is fierce, and each cell sabotages his neighbor's experiments and tries to be the first to break down the 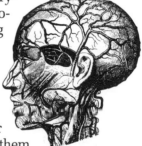 alcohol and look good to the Professor cell. But the Professor cell isn't helping them with their assignment, and it can take these cells over an hour to destroy the alcohol and congeners from just one beer.

So if you drink more than one beer an hour, you'll have some excess alcohol and congeners, which have time to travel all over your body and damage your cells. They destroy electrolytes, precious bodily fluids, and the eight essential vitamins and minerals you got from your breakfast cereal. In addition, the alcohol will wage guerrilla warfare on Mission Control—your brain. Your brain cells will be forced to surrender one by one, lobe by lobe, until all but a few vital brain centers function: those controlling heartbeat, respiration, copious urination, and the craving for food and sex.

Thus, alcohol not only trashes the chemical balance of your body, it also makes you act silly, eat too much, drink too much, and stay up too late. And, of course, none of this helps much the morning after. When you wake up, you are parched, your body and head ache from chemical imbalances, and you quiver, sway, and have trouble talking because your electrolytes are all screwed-up.

What can the drinker do to soften the blow? Well, we've found three opportune times to attend to hangovers. Each has its merits and drawbacks, as discussed below:

Before Drinking:

Remedial action before any alcohol enters your bloodstream shows impressive foresight. The advantage is that you are sober enough to carry out the remedy. The disadvantage is that such preventive action is basically useless. Medical practice suggests eating a large meal of fatty and oily foods and bread to line the stomach and slow the absorption of alcohol. Our practice: pizza.

Before Sleeping:

This is the most effective time to take action against the hangover. Unfortunately, you are usually too trashed to do anything but fall on your mattress. Medical practice suggests taking vitamins (especially B-12) and minerals and drinking water. Our practice is to get some late burgers, take two aspirin, chug as many glasses of water as possible, and crash.

After Waking:

Ideally, you have already done a lot to decrease your hangover, and you feel pretty good when you awake. Realistically, you are in pain. Medical practice suggests that you lie still in a dark room, sip soda water, take aspirin, and rest. Our practice is to chug two warm beers, throw on the Ray-Bans, eat lunch, and get psyched to do it again.

As you can tell, there are slight discrepancies between medically accepted hangover remedies and our practices. Though we don't guarantee that you'll live past 35 using our methods, at least they're more fun.

BIOLOGY LAB 101:

Perfecting the Power Chug

The art of chugging has always been shrouded in dark mystery, its secrets veiled to the uninitiated. Many non-chuggers perceive chugging as a miraculous feat of contortionism, a God-given ability, possessed by a lucky few, to inhale beer.

But these misguided sippers need not despair. Power chugging is an acquired trait, a skill to be learned, like riding a bicycle. Once done correctly, the power chug is never forgotten. The key to inhaling beer is the disciplined application of scientific principles—not luck, not genes.

Remember, too, that once you learn to chug, you need never again drink any liquid the traditional way. For years, parents and teachers have told us to drink politely—to swallow only small mouthfuls of liquid at a time. Try to undo this oppressive conditioning and teach yourself to guzzle without stopping to swallow. Be prepared to practice every day if necessary, until you develop "the feel."

The best time to practice is in the shower, just before a meal when your stomach is empty. Find a suitable cup and fill it with lukewarm water. Now, get psyched: relax your mouth, throat, and chest. Breathe deeply and slowly. Chant a mantra like, "Want that beer, want that beer." Bring the liquid to your lips. Tilt your head up only slightly; if you bend too much,

Limbering exercises can also help the power chugger.

your esophagus will constrict. Exhale fully and pour the water steadily into your mouth, more by tilting the cup and bending backward at the waist than by tilting your head. The goal is to achieve maximum throat dilation with the passage to the lungs closed (the physiological analog to woofing, but in reverse).

You may choke, sputter, and snarf the first few times, but that's because your airway is open and some water has decided to explore your lungs. The best way to develop proper technique is to imagine yourself swimming underwater in the ocean. As you break through the surface, a wave crashes on your face. Suddenly you have gulped a mass of water without even trying. The seawater rifled down your throat, and you didn't even swallow! This is the feeling you must recapture when you chug.

The ability to power chug has many practical applications. Only the most dedicated and most talented chuggers—the *foam de la foam* of chugging, so to speak—earn a position on a Yale Tang team. When we interviewed for jobs and graduate schools, we were often asked our chug times. In *Playboy*, the centerfold's Data Sheet will soon list the Playmate's chug times. Future Presidential debates will require candidates to chug on national TV.

Competent power chugging is just one of those things that determine whether you "make the grade." It's a trait shared by top beer gamesters and world leaders around the globe.

MUSIC 120:

Beer in Classical Music

Classical music is a lot like sea urchin roe. Both are enjoyed by small groups of aesthetes trying to demonstrate their superior taste. Take opera, for example. Who really enjoys watching a fat guy warble in a foreign language to some heifer who looks like Miss Piggy?

However, not all pre-rock music can be dismissed so quickly. In fact, many old songs are filled with tales of fun folks having good times. And their enjoyment, then as now, often included the golden sauce.

Our national anthem, for instance, was not always concerned with "bombs bursting in air." Francis Scott Key actually borrowed the tune from the theme song of a British men's club, whose members were determined to get bombed in a different manner. The original song had nothing to do with "the home of the brave." Instead, it ends with a toast, proposing that the club members should "intwine...with Bacchus's vine."

But even that poses a problem. This tune, rousing as it may have been, perpetuates the erroneous view that wine is more sophisticated than beer. Just as many socialites today prefer Château Effete over a cold Bud, so too did many drinkers of yore regard beer as a beverage of the unwashed hordes.

Luckily, many songwriters have exhibited a clearer understanding of beer's importance. Bedrich Smetana, a 19th-century Czech composer, reveals such insight in his opera *The Bartered Bride:*

You foam within our glasses, you lusty golden brew.
Whoever imbibes will take fire from you.
The young and the old sing your praises.
Here's to beer! Here's to cheer! Here's to beer!

Medieval monks especially valued their beer. The pious, celibate image we have of monks only disguised the lusty truth: monasteries in the Dark Ages were equivalent to today's fraternity houses. The brethren may have served God, but they also served lots of beevo. Johann Schein, a 16th-century German composer, reveals the advanced level of drinking technique found in the monasteries. Note especially the proper chugging form:

So my fellow friars, who wants to be sad now?
Sing, play! We must have good cheer.
With such good beer... bottoms up!
Empty it in one swift gulp.
The glass must be entirely inverted.

A number of composers shared a common view about the place of women in drinking society. Women, they believed, should not be sober independents or mere house slaves, content to be inebriated with love for their men. No, women should be good drinking buddies. This attitude is suggested in the famous aria *Back and Side Go Bare:*

And Tib my wife, that as her life
Loveth well good ale to seek.
Full oft drinks she, tell ye may see
The tears run down her cheek.

While on the subject of love, many know the tune of Maurice Ravel's *Bolero*, Bo Derek's musical aphrodisiac. Ravel also dealt with more liquid forms of fulfillment. Spurning the pseudo-sophisticated, sherry-sipping school of drinking, Ravel's *Drinking Song* proposed a no-nonsense rationale for sucking down those beers:

> *I drink to joy!*
> *Joy is the one aim*
> *to which I go straight when I am drunk.*

Ravel should have been pals with Beethoven. When Ludwig Von finished a tough day of distilling the human experience into entirely unique musical forms, he liked to hike to the corner pub and sample another product of distillation. Though unable to win free games on baroque pinball machines, Beethoven reveals in his song *Come Fill* that he knew how to do a 12-ounce curl:

> *Come fill, fill, my good fellow!*
> *Fill high, high, my good fellow!*
> *And let's be merry and mellow,*
> *And let us have one bottle more...*
> *Huzzah! then for one bottle more!*

Though Ravel and Beethoven have not composed for some time (in fact, they are decomposing), their musical love for beer thrives in many college drinking songs. *The Stein Song* of the University of Michigan is a fine example. Note the unforced lyricism of the rhyme scheme and the subtle dialectic between assonance and consonance in the final line:

> *Michigan, Michigan, may your glory never pale.*
> *To your prosperity, we drink down our ale.*
> *May our sons of future years, like their dads today,*
> *Whooper up for Michigan, hooray, hooray, hooray!*

Despite such rousing lyrics, we think the art of the drinking song reached its zenith in the 19th century. For instance, even though *The Morning After* admits that beer can affect your system like Drano, it shows that the true drinking enthusiast always has the ability to rally:

A heated interior, a wobbly bed,
A seasick man with an aching head;
Whiskey, beer, gin, booze galore,
Were introduced to the cuspidor!

And with morning came bags of ice
So very necessary in this life of vice;

And when I calmed my throbbing brain,
Did I swear off and quit?
No, I got soused again.

In sum, we hope we have demonstrated that composers, like their brother writers and playwrights, arc partiers, too. With all this evidence, it should be quite clear why everybody sings when they're trashed.

SOCIOLOGY 125:

Beer—The Social Lubricant

Beer makes you drunk. It also makes you, uh, horny, and a hangover may not be the only thing you wake up with the next morning. In addition, beer has the uncanny ability to decrease your aesthetic judgment by shocking degrees. Remember Baker's Law: At 3:00 a.m., when you're really trashed, everybody looks attractive.

When sober, most of us are initially attracted to those in the 7 to 10 range. After a few beers, we might even have the courage to approach them. But as the beers go down, so do aesthetic standards—precipitously, as demonstrated below:

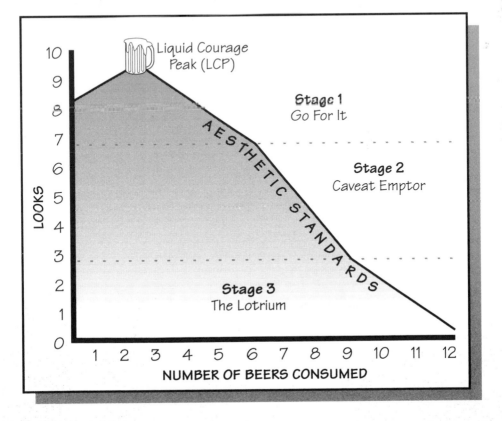

After a six-pack or so, you enter the *Caveat Emptor* ("Let the buyer beware") stage, and people normally considered plain (the 3 to 6 range) start to look pretty good. You just have to hope that none of your friends are around to remind you otherwise the next morning.

Late in the evening, after way too much liquid courage, some unfortunate people pass into the dreaded *Lotrium* level. ("Lotrium" is a Bantu word meaning, loosely, "snorting, hairy beast.") Encounters at this stage are disgusting but excusable,  because they are symptoms of a myopia known as "night blindness," which can lead to an even more distressing plight, the Coyote Morning (which occurs when you awake after a binge and discover that the person sleeping on your arm is so repulsive that you would rather chew it off than chance waking him/her when you leave). The pain of a Coyote Morning and the risk of contracting something awful are enough to make even the most promiscuous hoser think twice.

Danger: Lotrium

On the brighter side of such rude awakenings is the fact that sexual activity can burn a lot of pounds off your beer gut:

One hour of	Burns
scoping/swooping	1 beer
visual foreplay	3 beers
heavy groveling	5 beers
scrumping	10 beers
post-coital regret	15 beers

A case of night blindness can actually get you into good shape! In fact, one lustful night of requited concupiscence can burn off a whole weekend of beer gaming. And this doesn't include all the weight you'll sweat off trying to explain to your "steady" why you weren't home all night. But what the hell—it'll make a great story some day.

ENGLISH 109:
Non-Fiction Writing

"The Day I Entered a Fern Bar and Lived to Tell about It"

I had stayed up all night playing beer games, and I awoke the next afternoon with a manly hangover and a stomach in desperate need of solid nutrition. So, in search of a good cheeseburger and a tall, cool brew, I wandered aimlessly, shielding my eyes from the sunset, and walked into a place that seemed like a decent eating establishment.

Man, was I wrong. I barely left with my hormones intact.

As I entered, my senses were assaulted by a deluge of brass, brick, stained glass, and hanging plants. Annoyed but too hung over to care, I slumped down at a table. Suddenly, a waitress materialized. "I'm sorry, sir, but you'll have to wait to be seated," she said officiously. As she led  me back to the bar, leaves and twigs brushed my face menacingly. I was told to wait by a tank full of tropical fish.

Trying to make the best of things, I decided to find the jukebox. Maybe I'll crank some tunes and cheer this place up, I thought. But just then, a Barry Manilow song slithered from an overhead speaker. No *real* jukebox has Barry Manilow songs, I realized. A quick glance through the red and green drinks on the bar confirmed my fears. The bartender had just put Barry's *Greatest Hits* into a concealed tape deck.

Seven nauseating songs later, I was led to a table beside a large window, ensuring that every pedestrian could watch me eat. A wispy-looking waiter waltzed over, lit the candle on the table, and sang, "Hi, my name is David, and I'll be your host for the evening." *Host?* "Can I get you a drink?" he continued. "You look as though you're thirsty for a wine spritzer. Or perhaps one of our fresh-fruit daiquiris?" He grinned.

I still didn't fully understand the situation, but my natural instincts put me on the defensive.

"Cheeseburger. Budweiser," I said. I was not smiling back.

David sauntered off and, 20 minutes later, still bored and beerless, I decided to eavesdrop on the couple at the next table. They seemed to be engaged in a serious conversation:

"Look, Mark, you're just not, like, growing with me. You don't, like, understand my needs. I really, like, have to explore the range of my personality."

"But, Brooke—"

"No, Mark, I need my own, like, space, my own, like, identity. I have to find out who I am."

"But, Brooke—"

"I'm sorry, Mark, but I'm, like, really into honesty, you know? Our relationship is, like, too dysfunctional."

"But, Brooke—"

I was amazed that people could utter such pablum. Where was I, anyway? My hangover was subsiding, and I was finally beginning to understand my predicament when David arrived with my order. "Enjoy!" he said, with a flurry of gesticulations. "If there's anything you need, just whistle."

God.

My "cheeseburger" was actually a beef patty—no bun—smothered in bleu cheese and sauteed mushrooms. And served in a wicker basket, no less.

My rejuvenated brain cells suddenly put the pieces of this gruesome puzzle together—hanging plants, Barry Manilow, sensitivity-speak—I had walked into a fern bar! I knew that if I didn't get out of there fast, the aroma of the plants would affect my powers of reason and good taste, and I'd soon be ordering piña colada wine coolers and spinach quiche.

I chugged most of my beer, poured the rest on the candle, laid a ten on the table, and made a power dash for the door.

I stumbled onto the sidewalk and inhaled the evening air with relief. I had escaped, and, most important, none of my friends had seen me in the window. I headed straight for Rudy's, where I could get a real cheeseburger. Raw.

BOOT FACTOR FOUR

I n **Boot Factor Four games**, there are no winners, only sur-
vivors. At B.F. 4, the best you can hope for is to avoid being
the sap who passes out or tosses cookies. Boot Factor Four
competitors have applied acquired gaming skill and technique
to sustain the ravages of these grueling contests. These remarkable athletes sample the bittersweet pleasure of advanced beer-
gaming: the thrill of victory and the agony of a probable cleans-
ing at the foot of the big, white telephone to God.

Beer-an-Inning

Yards

Shot-a-Minute

Acey-Deucey

Caps

Hi-Lo

Red-Black

Dimes

Bladder Bust

Beer Pong

Volley Pong

Blow Pong

Beer-an-Inning

Boot Factor: 4

Baseball is a great American pastime. Drinking beer is a great American pastime. So what could be more logical than combining baseball and beer drinking? What—besides peanuts, Cracker Jack, and covering the point spread—could make a wholesome outing to the ballpark better but a thoroughly unwholesome beer game?

Whenever we're in the cheap seats, we like to play **Beer-an-Inning**. The rules are simple: Start every inning with a full cup of beer. Finish it by the end of the inning.

A leisurely task, many might assume. Don't kid yourselves. Though it is acceptable to drink 12-ounce beers, it is preferable, indeed sporting, to use the 16-, 20-, or 24-ounce models. And since **Beer-an-Inning** is usually played at live ball games, you must drink whatever swill the stadium sells. (Playing **Beer-an-Inning** to a game on television is permissible only if you use really cheap beer.)

As innings shoot by, pacing becomes essential. If you leave too much beer for the bottom half, you risk a rapid chug if the inning ends quickly. Double plays can be devastating. Extra innings can be catastrophic. Doubleheaders? Don't even think about it.

Luckily for beer gamers, unforeseen lulls occur in any match: an extended manager-umpire confrontation or a little rain, for example. Without breaks like these, only the "seventh inning retch" keeps **Beer-an-Inning** players from hitting the showers early.

Beer-an-Inning can be a lot of fun for fans and players alike.

Yards

Boot Factor: 4

Resembling a form of medieval torture more than a beer game, **Yards** pits contestants against the clock to see who can drink a lot of beer from a weird-looking glass the fastest.

A yard glass, found in most high-class bars like brewpubs and such, contains 2.5 pints of beer. The glass, which is three feet long (duh), has a bowl at the bottom and a long, fluted neck. This design makes it tough to drink the last few ounces of beer without pouring it all over yourself—a *faux pas* that, of course, earns the sloppy yardster a penalty drink.

Avid yard drinkers have developed several techniques to alleviate the problem of chugging those last ounces. The most popular is to spin the yard slowly as you drink, thus preventing a vacuum from forming in the bowl as the liquid leaves. Another method was created by the legendary "Boot" Strapp, who could toss back a yard in ten seconds. Strapp jammed the open end of the glass into his mouth and then just opened his throat. Although his technique is considered the most effective, it has never been duplicated.

Normal people will need 15-30 seconds to drink a half-yard. A full yard will take a good bit longer because the glass is much more difficult to handle.

Trivia buffs take note: The yard glass can be traced back to the reign of James I of England in the early 1600's. Also, the former Prime Minister of Australia, Bob Hawke, once held the world record for emptying the contents of a yard. As a student at Oxford, Hawke drained one in 12 seconds. The current record-holder is Englishman Peter Dowdeswell, who polished off a full yard of ale in a mere five seconds!

Shot-a-Minute

Boot Factor: 4

Anyone who entertains the idea of doing a shot of beer every minute for an hour is truly a gaming fanatic. **Shot-a-Minute** is that simple: each player has one minute to consume a one-ounce shot of beer, and he must do so every minute for a full hour. No sweat, huh? Guess again, big guy.

For those who think **Shot-a-Minute** is for wimps, there's **The Century Club**. Players drink a one-ounce shot of beer every minute for 100 minutes. This works out to over eight beers per person, which doesn't seem too strenuous on paper. But anyone who tries it will know differently. To make it especially tough, don't allow anyone to go to the bathroom until the game is over.

"It is the hour to be drunken! To escape being martyred slaves of time, be ceaselessly drunk!"
Charles Baudelaire

Acey-Deucey

Boot Factor: 4

Acey-Deucey is a classic beer game: moronically easy and a whole lot of fun. All you need is a deck of cards, beer, and some thirsty players.

To begin, the dealer gives each player two cards face up. The players then bet one, two, or three shots of beer against the dealer that the third card will be a value in-between the first two.

For instance, if the player has a three and a seven, he would have to draw a four, five, or six to win. Since the odds of doing so are not great, he would probably bet only one or two shots. If the player wins, the dealer must do the shots immediately. If the player loses, he drinks. Needless to say, a contestant volunteers to deal only if he has a chronic beer deficiency.

We should note that the first player decides whether aces are high or low, and his decision dictates the status of the ace for the rest of the round. Also, if two successive cards are dealt (e.g., a six and a seven), the player must drink a shot.

Caps

Boot Factor: 4

Caps is so popular on campus these days that it's more accurately labeled an intramural sport. Although the concept is simple—throw a bottle cap into a cup of beer to make your opponent drink—the effects can be devastating.

Sit on the floor facing your opponent, legs in front and spread apart. Your feet must touch your opponent's feet, forming a diamond-shaped playing area. Next, place a cup filled with beer a few inches in front of your crotch; your opponent must do the same. You then throw a bottle cap in any fashion and try to make it land in your opponent's cup.

If the throw is successful, your opponent chugs one-third or one-half of his beer. If the cap hits the rim of the cup but does not go in, you may re-throw. If you hit three rim shots on any one turn, you must forfeit your throw and take a penalty drink. After a successful throw, you can play one of two ways. Either the winner gets to toss again, or the loser tosses.

Games are played to 11, 15, or 21 points and are always "win by two." You may lean as far forward as you can, but *no*

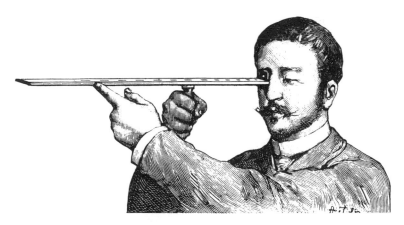

Professional Caps players use sophisticated targeting devices.

bending the knees. By the way, if Manute Bol challenges you to a quick game of **Caps**, we advise you to decline respectfully.

Numerous tossing styles exist, but only three are consistently successful: backhand, freestyle, and the slam dunk. When you're on defense, the ability to wiggle your pelvis in an obscene fashion, hoot and holler, and make utterly foolish faces often proves effective in distracting your opponent during his toss. It's also important to know when to move your cup, since it can be placed anywhere inside the "diamond."

The ability to make foolish faces is a real asset in Caps.

In any case, whenever a full cup appears on the playing field, you should always throw with excessive velocity in order to splash beer all over your opponent's groin. It's always good for a laugh.

"Doth it not show vilely in me to desire small beer?"
William Shakespeare, *Henry IV, Part II*

Hi-Lo

Boot Factor: 4

The next three games—**Hi-Lo**, **Red-Black**, and **Dimes**—were all developed in direct response to criticism that beer games are too complicated for the hopelessly drunk. Well, for those never-say-die partiers, **Hi-Lo** is the answer.

Hi-Lo, which requires only that players be able to recognize shapes and colors, is played with a deck of cards divided evenly among the competitors. Each player turns over one card at a time. Those with low cards drink for every card higher than theirs.

For example, if three people are playing, the player with the lowest card drinks twice, the player with the middle card drinks once, and the player with the highest card does not drink at all. Ties are settled by suit; spades are high, then hearts, diamonds, and clubs.

If this doesn't sound too complex, even for the incredibly trashed, just wait until it's time to shuffle. This task usually proves much too difficult, and the game ends.

Red-Black

Boot Factor: 4

Even simpler to play than **Hi-Lo**, **Red-Black** is the easiest beer game to learn and teach, and it's the quickest game to play. Thus, it's ideal when you need a game to pass the time between classes, while waiting for a date, during TV commercials, etc.

In **Red-Black**, two players place a deck of cards face down and draw from the top. If the card is red, you drink. If it's black, your opponent drinks.

It shouldn't take a genius to realize that there are 26 red cards and 26 black cards in a deck. This means that each player will drink 13 beers during his trip through the deck (if traditional half-beer penalties are observed). If your competitive instinct demands that there be a winner, remove one card before starting.

Dimes

Boot Factor: 4

Played long enough, **Dimes** will make small change of even die-hard gamesters. There's no disguising your purpose here. You want to get trashed, and you want to get trashed *now*. With **Dimes**, the Power Drunk is no problem.

Luckily, the game is ridiculously simple. One of two players claims heads or tails and flips three dimes so that they land on the table. For every coin that comes up in his favor, his opponent must drink a shot of beer. For every losing coin, the tosser drinks. Players alternate tossing. We're talking minimal strategy here.

Strange as it may seem, **Dimes** works equally well with quarters, nickels, and pennies.

Bladder Bust

Boot Factor: 4

Bladder Bust is as simple as **The 100 Beer Club** (see page 134), and just as demented.

Any number of people sit in a closed room. Each must drink a bottle of beer every five minutes. The first person who leaves the room for any reason loses. The last person left in the room wins.

That's it. Sick, huh?

Beer Pong

Boot Factor: 4

Traditionally, Ping-Pong has been associated with adroit Chinese and low-budget resorts. The simple addition of beer, however, transforms this rather lame pastime into an exciting and rewarding pursuit.

Beer Pong begins with each player placing his full cup on the center line of the table, about one foot from the back edge. The players flip a coin to see who will serve, and play commences with the normal Ping-Pong rules in effect (21 points per game, win by two, best two out of three games, etc.). Throughout the match, each player tries to hit his opponent's cup with the ball. If a player's cup is struck, he must drink a certain amount of beer, depending on how and where the cup was hit.

There are four sips per cup, and the penalties are as follows:

Infraction:	*Drink Penalty:*
hit side of cup after bounce or on the fly	one sip
hit rim of cup after bounce or on the fly	two sips
hit cup on serve	server drinks two sips
ball lands in cup after bounce	three sips
ball lands in cup on the fly	chug rest of beer
ball knocks cup over (fly or bounce)	refill cup and chug
player knocks his own cup over	refill cup and chug
loser of game	chug full beer

Remember, if a ball hits or bounces off any part of the cup and has not bounced on the table more than once, it is still in play. This rule creates the chance for multiple penalties within a single point. In such a case, the penalties are dispensed in the order they occurred. Note that it is illegal to hit your opponent's cup on your serve, and playing at the net to protect your cup is really wimpy.

Beer Pong for doubles is identical to singles except that two cups per team are used. Players should place their cups one foot from the table's edge and one foot from either side of the center line. The players on each team must alternate returning the shots as they rally.

As play continues, brain cells, memory, and motor coordination discontinue. But **Beer Pong** athletes should always try to remember two effective shots. One is the drop shot, which lands just over the net and dies. It often causes your opponent to lunge for the return, upsetting his own beer in the process. Another strategic shot is the deep lob, since it's likely to drop in your opponent's cup on the fly. But be careful—if your lob is too short, you risk a punishing return and a beer *tsunami*. Bring many mung kimonos to clean up the mess.

"Better belly burst than good liquor be lost."
Jonathan Swift

Volley Pong

Boot Factor: 4

Volley Pong, a tougher form of **Beer Pong**, was developed, we suspect, by the Dartmouth fraternity system. We tried it on a road trip to Hanover, New Hampshire on a football weekend and nearly tossed our tacos. Fortunately, our football team kicked Dartmouth's butt.

Volley Pong is for doubles only. Place two cups of beer side by side (touching) on the center line of the Ping-Pong table, approximately one foot from the back edge. Flip a coin to see who gets to receive first. Serving is a disadvantage. If a player hits the other team's cup on the serve, his team must take a pair of healthy gulps.

Once the serve is properly in play, the action resembles volleyball more than Ping-Pong. The receiving player "sets" or hits the ball into the air towards his teammate, who then slams or "spikes" the ball in the direction of the opponent's cups. If he misses but still hits the table, the other team can retrieve and volley in the same manner. But if they can't handle the slam and miss the ball, then they must serve. If the slamming player misses the table altogether, his team must serve. Should he hit the cups on the slam, the other players must down one-third of their beers. If a cup gets knocked over, the players must refill their beers, drink them, and wipe up the mess. All games are played to 21, win by two, and mung rags are a must.

Volley Pong makes a great spectator sport. Feel free to import sand and cheering, nubile, bikini-clad women to enhance the atmosphere.

Blow Pong

Boot Factor: 4

Blow Pong is the only beer game that should be considered for Olympic competition. Few games are as well-suited for settling heated rivalries: fraternity against fraternity, boys against girls, lawyers against normal, decent people, etc.

The object of **Blow Pong** is to blow a Ping-Pong ball off the side of a table guarded by another team, thus forcing them to drink. **Blow Pong** boasts an enticingly high Boot Factor because of its punishing combination of imbibition and hyperventilation.

The first step in **Blow Pong** is to prepare the equipment. For best results, remove the net on a Ping-Pong table and tape the seam to create a uniform rolling surface. Otherwise, use any fairly large table. Next, get a supply of Ping-Pong balls and choose two teams. Each team claims a long side and short end of the table to defend and kneels around it. The ball is then dropped into the table, and blowing begins. The team that blows the ball off its opponent's side scores a point, and the scored-upon team must drink a specified amount. A game is played to 21 (win by two), and a match is the best of three (or five).

If there are not enough players to form two teams, we suggest you try one-on-one play. Each player chooses a place at the table and uses two bottles or cups to define his goal. The rules of play are otherwise identical to team play.

Your natural ability to blow forcefully for a long time cannot be improved, short of learning to play the tuba, but certain techniques can help. First, don't allow your cheeks to puff out Dizzy Gillespie-style, as this contributes to loss of lip control, which leads to spraying and sputtering. Aside from transmitting miscellaneous diseases, sputtering at the **Blow Pong** table is simply gross. Second, the power for the blow should emanate low in the belly, creating a sensation not unlike that leading to a good heave.

Now, a few words on **Blow Pong** etiquette. Only ball hogs lean over the table. Leaning is *déclassé,* and the rule against breaking the vertical plane of the table must be enforced strictly. The best way to avoid a "face fault" is to maintain chin contact with the table edge. Also, a team loses the point if the ball touches any part of a player. Since the lips and nose are the most commonly hit areas, touching the ball is known as "getting faced." Because **Blow Pong** is a gentleman's game based on a strict code of honor, a player hit by the ball is duty-bound to end the point immediately by confessing.

The key strategy in **Blow Pong** is to determine the weak link in the opponent's line of defense. Invariably, one player is a little too hammered, too spastic, or too inexperienced to stop laughing uncontrollably. This person is instantly pegged as the "black hole," a player who, literally, sucks. A smart team will concentrate on blowing him into the arms of the porcelain god.

We are developing a **Blow Pong** Hall of Fame, which now includes Louis Armstrong, Ethel Merman, Puff the Magic Dragon, Moby Dick, Jabba the Hut, Linda Lovelace, and Monica Lewinsky. Feel free to send us your nominations.

Champion Blow Pong players begin training at age 7.

Twenty-Five Movies to Drink to: A Few Mindless Classics

1. Animal House
2. Fast Times at Ridgemont High
3. The Rocky Horror Picture Show
4. Strange Brew
5. Pulp Fiction (*not mindless, but great anyway*)
6. Grease
7. Porky's
8. Wayne's World
9. Saturday Night Fever
10. Bill and Ted's Excellent Adventure
11. The Blues Brothers
12. Barbarella (*Jane Fonda in a see-through spacesuit*)
13. Ferris Bueller's Day Off
14. Caddyshack
15. Eraserhead
16. Plan 9 from Outer Space
17. Enter the Dragon
18. Metropolitan (*only because you can see Scott dancing in a conga line*)
19. Ghostbusters
20. Apocalypse Now (*only if you fast-forward while Brando rambles on about T. S. Eliot*)
21. any Tarzan movie with Johnny Weismuller
22. any James Bond movie (*Sean Connery preferred*)
18. any Clint Eastwood movie (*except Bridges of Madison County*)
24. any Ronald Reagan movie
25. Mars Needs Women

BOOT FACTOR FIVE

If the **Boot Factor Four gamester** lives close to the edge, the Boot Factor Five player has jumped. He accepts the fact that the Big Ralph is imminent. His only question is when to employ the reverse drink strategically in order to outlast fellow Neanderthals. Generally speaking, if a B.F. 5 player does not voluntarily hurl, he will involuntarily barf later in the game. Such a gross *faux pas* merits immediate disqualification and, of course, a penalty chug.

Beer Hunter

Kill the Keg

Tending the Teat

Slush Fund

The 100 Beer Club

Boot-a-Bout

Beer Hunter

Boot Factor: 5

Beer Hunter is for the truly hard core. The game parodies the intense Russian roulette scenes in the movie about Vietnam veterans, *The Deer Hunter.* Hence the name.

To simulate the ambiance of the smoky, back room betting gallery in Saigon, play some Asian-sounding music—or at least something menacing—softly in the background. Players should dress in fatigues and use rolled bandannas or neckties as headbands. Everyone should approach the gaming area with absolute seriousness. It will turn hilarious soon enough.

The two players, led into the room blindfolded, are placed facing each other at a table. The referee then, with great fanfare, shows the spectators a new six-pack of beer cans, holding it high over his head. He removes each beer from its ring and places them all on the table between the players. He then takes one of the cans and shakes it up very hard. He places this can back on the table amongst the unshaken cans, and he shuffles the cans around so that no spectator knows which one is the shaken can. If they wish, the spectators may now bet beer on which player will "survive."

When the betting is over, the referee removes the players' blindfolds and asks one of them to choose a can from the "ammo dump." The referee then spins an empty can on the table, and the player at whom the top of the can is pointing must go first. The player picks up the can, places it directly under his nostrils, and pops the top. If the player hesitates before pulling the top, the judge must berate him by yelling, *"Mao! Mao!"* in his face. If the player pulls the top and discovers that he does not have the "loaded" can, he then places his beer down, and his opponent must choose from the five remaining cans and repeat the procedure.

This intense activity continues until one of the players commits nasal suicide (i.e., gets the shaken can) and drenches himself. This losing player must drink what's left of his

Robert DeNiro in The Deer Hunter.

"loaded" beer and then leave the table to work on drinking *all* the other beers opened in that round.

The surviving player is then re-blindfolded, and another contestant, also blindfolded, is led into the room. The referee repeats the routine with another six-pack, and the new round begins.

Beer Hunter, of course, can be modified to accommodate up to six players. Remember, the loser must drink all open beers.

Obviously, **Beer Hunter**, like the movie, is a game suited only to those with nerves of steel. Those who hesitate will face a barrage of *"Mao!"* from the referee—probably more disgraceful than losing. Also, of course, **Beer Hunter** should be played with small cans of beer, since few would survive the explosion of a tall boy.

And remember, all those who play **Beer Hunter** will get wet. Very, very wet. But the sensation of beer-sodden clothes and the smell of stale brew against your skin ought to exhilarate true beer hunters, making them feel as though they fought a desperate battle against the forces of evil—and won. Wear the wet clothes with undying pride long into the night.

"There is nothing for a case of nerves like a case of beer."

Joan Goldstein

Kill the Keg

Boot Factor: 5

Kill the Keg, a sacred ritual at keg parties, serves to separate the hearty quaffers from the lightweights, as well as polish off unfinished kegs. After all, there is no excuse for leftover beer.

A round of **Kill the Keg** is required when a keg party begins to die. This usually occurs at one of two times. Either the party has become overpopulated with the pompous cocktail crowd that finds verbal communication preferable to body language and massive swilling (an attitude utterly ill-suited to the traditional beer blast). Or, the majority of guests have simply wimped out, passed out, or gone home. In either case, per capita beer consumption has declined to a level that would embarrass even the residents of Utah.

When the cry "Rally!" is sounded, die-hard partiers must gather around the aluminum provider and take turns filling their cups and drinking. Once a certain filling order is established, it may not be broken. Thus, as the last person in line fills up his beer, the first must have finished his and be ready to refill. This continues until the keg is dead. (Note: Be sure to enlist a weightlifter-type to pump the keg constantly and maintain a steady stream of beer.)

There are two cardinal rules in **Kill the Keg**: 1. The tap must never be closed, and 2. no beer can be spilled or wasted. The only way to slow the rate of consumption and give players a break to belch, breathe, and generally re-group is to add more players. As the game progresses and severe abdominal distension claims player after player, new recruits become the key to success. But remember, it is *sacrilege* to close the tap.

If things get really rough, we suggest using the Heimlich Boot Maneuver on fellow players (a scene unfortunately cut from *Animal House*) to make room for more beer.

For the Health-Conscious Gamester

BOSTON (Reuters)—People who drink moderate amounts of beer, wine or other liquor daily halve their heart-attack risk, a study in the *New England Journal of Medicine* says.

The research, published December 12, 1993, confirmed previous large-scale studies that have shown a lower risk of heart disease among moderate drinkers. "There now seems little doubt that alcohol exerts a protective effect against coronary disease," Drs. Gary Friedman and Arthur Klatsky wrote in an editorial.

The study of 680 volunteers, half of whom had suffered a heart attack, found a 50% reduction of heart seizure risk if they consumed a drink or two daily. Three or more drinks offered no additional benefit. The alcohol increases the levels of "good cholesterol" in the blood known as HDL.

Tending the Teat

Boot Factor: 5

More than a beer game, **Tending the Teat** is a heroic feat requiring remarkable intestinal fortitude—and remarkable intestines. **Tending the Teat** is a contest—no, an *event*—in which participants go head-to-head with the stiffest competition imaginable: the keg. **Tending the Teat** is next of kin to **Kill the Keg**, but it is generally more daring, more studly, and more sick.

To play **Tending the Teat**, you must choose a referee and an Honorary Beer Wench. The Wench is responsible for keeping the keg pumped so that beer flows out of the tap (the "teat") at a constant rate. The referee is responsible for presenting the rules, monitoring the game, announcing the winner, and knowing CPR.

Players gather around the keg, and the first player affixes his mouth to the tap. If the keg has the usual vertical tap, this may require some contortionist maneuvers to achieve relative comfort. Typically, the sumo wrestler, squat/straddle style seems to be most effective in achieving both comfort and maximum throat dilation.

When the player is ready, the referee places two or three fingers lightly on the player's Adam's apple. The Wench opens the tap, and the player swallows mouthful after mouthful, with the referee counting each gulp aloud as the drinker's Adam's apple bobs up and down. The point is to chalk up as many swallows as possible before drooling, snarfing, spewing, or passing out. When the player can swallow no longer, he dismounts the keg and retires to the crowd to watch the next challenger.

When all contestants have had their fill, the referee announces the winner and brings—or drags—him before the cheering masses to be properly lauded. A date with the Beer Wench and/or the porcelain god usually follows.

Even More Expressions for Getting Sick

1. call the dinosaurs
2. three-dimensional burp
3. unload your cargo
4. bark at your john
5. yell for Europe
6. polish your tonsils
7. upward nutritional mobility
8. dance with your tub
9. hang a food rope
10. blow a quarter pounder
11. repeat dinner
12. yell cabbage
13. howl
14. zuke

Slush Fund

Boot Factor: 5

Being dedicated gamblers, we decided there should be some way to play beer games and win money at the same time. Thus, we took it upon ourselves to invent **Slush Fund**.

In **Slush Fund**, players must pay to drink. (Of course, avid beer gamesters— notorious for knowing myriad schemes to mooch free beer—will cringe at the idea of paying to drink, but this is a great game, so just get over it.) To begin, someone brings a full pitcher to a group at a table. Whoever starts must buy ·the privilege of drinking by dropping a quarter into the pitcher. He then "owns" the pitcher and may drink as much as he wants, directly from the pitcher. (Glasses are too civilized for this game.) After drinking, he passes the pitcher to the next player, who must also ante-up. After he deposits a quarter, he, too, may drink as much as he wishes.

At any time, whoever owns the pitcher may take all the money at the bottom—as long as he drinks all the beer.

The strategy of **Slush Fund** becomes obvious quickly. Each drinker who decides not to pursue the money will drink just a sip. The quarters will accumulate, and the pitcher will remain virtually full. Whoever decides to "drink for dollars" will be facing a lot of beer. Inevitably, somebody will decide, uncoerced, that approximately $2.75 is adequate compensation for booting. That's beautiful, if you think about it.

Economics majors are usually stars at this game, with their keen sense of opportunity cost and supply and demand. History majors, on the other hand, never seem to learn the lessons of the past.

The 100 Beer Club

Boot Factor: 5

Membership in **The 100 Beer Club** is free and open to all, though we certainly don't encourage it. Although the requirements for admission are simple, few are twisted enough to gain entry. All you need is a spare weekend and, oh, 100 beers or so. Got the idea?

Those warped enough even to consider joining the Club have from midnight Thursday until midnight Sunday to finish 100 12-ounce beers. (After all, weekends were made for Michelob.) That works out to one beer every 43 minutes—if you stay awake for the duration. If you can count 100 empties at midnight on Sunday, you are an official member of the Club. Of course, if you can count *anything* on Sunday, you're doing pretty good.

Applicants to the Club perform best when they begin their quest with a large group of friends—that is, many friends, or simply large friends, like the football team. Peer pressure is very effective in keeping the drop-out rate low, though not much can be done about the pass-out rate. In any case, for those choosing this awesome task, we advise discipline, a steady pace, and a physician's phone number.

Boot-a-Bout

Boot Factor: 5

Boot-a-Bout is for animals. Of course, we mean this as a compliment. In **Boot-a-Bout**, there are no winners. Players lose either their money or their lunch. Fortunately for exceptional gamesters, it is at least possible to salvage your reputation.

The beauty of **Boot-a-Bout** lies in its simplicity. The game, which must be played in a bar, begins with one player buying a pitcher. He initiates the round by sipping from the pitcher and passing it to his right. The game continues like this, with each player drinking as much as he wants and then passing the chalice of golden ambrosia.

There is only one rule, so read carefully. The player who drank just *before* the player who finishes the pitcher must buy the next pitcher and start the next round.

If this sounds dull, think again. Many players will go to extraordinary lengths to avoid paying for the next pitcher. In fact, the pitcher rarely gets even half-empty before some gorilla goes for it. Some Cro-Magnons have been known to pound the whole pitcher right off the bat.

Of course, if you chug the pitcher, you'll probably have to reverse drink in the nearest bathroom if you want to play another round. André the Giant might have been able to hold a quick pitcher or two in his estimable gut, but we mere mortals cannot.

A word about technique: An experienced **Boot-a-Bout** player knows how much the next player can drink and how much he has drunk already. As this differential approaches zero, a good player will taunt the next player by drinking just enough beer to make the pitcher look tempting.

We recommend that everyone play **Boot-a-Bout** at least once, just to know the anguish of clutching that 75%-full vessel. Should you pass it? Is the guy next to you psyched to pound it? Or should you go for it? Do you really mind blowing doughnuts? Why are you doing this, anyway?

Ah, we seldom feel such raw emotional intensity in these sterilized, technologically advanced times. Of all beer games, only **Boot-a-Bout** gives birth to existential dilemmas. What prompts you to play such a game in a civilized world where no one is actually forcing you to? Why would you choose to puke when you don't have to? Why do you go to such great lengths to avoid paying a few bucks for a pitcher of beer, when you gladly spend thousands on burritos, lame movies, and college? If these questions are as baffling to you as they are to us, then we suggest you head down to the local bar to play a few rounds of **Boot-a-Bout** tonight. Drop us a line if you come up with any answers.

Twenty Post-Game Activities

1. Wear six-pack cartons like party hats.
2. Chow pizza.
3. Wake up wimp roommates.
4. Go pickle-bobbing at the local deli.
5. Play air guitars.
6. Melt bottles in the fireplace.
7. Rearrange parked cars.
8. Steal road signs.
9. Break something you didn't need.
10. Break something your roommate did need.
11. Crank obnoxious music loud enough to disturb your neighbors.
12. Go cow-tipping.
13. Have a fire extinguisher fight.
14. Men: Try to pick up girls at a party (while wearing #1, of course).
15. Women: Try to pick up guys at a party (also while wearing #1, of course). (Actually, save yourself a lot of trouble and just look for guys wearing #1.)
16. See how much noise a keg makes bouncing down the stairs.
17. Sing off-key.
18. Test the laws of gravity by throwing stuff out the window.
19. Blow chow.
20. Pass out.

Good Stuff to Buy!

The Complete Book of Beer Drinking Games. Well, uh, it's the book you're reading _now_, so clearly it's funny and cool and all that. And if your friends keep swiping your copy, then buy a bunch more and give them as gifts. **$8.95**

Beer Games 2: The Exploitative Sequel. If you like the book in your hands now, you'll _love_ the sequel. There's over 40 great new games, plus more funny essays and lists— and the hilarious Beer Catalog! **$8.95**

The Hangover Handbook. With over 100 cures for the gamester's scourge, this book combines humor and real hangover remedies that will have you back in party mode fast. Face it— if you've got our two guides to beer games, you'll need this book. **$8.95**

TO ORDER, CALL 800-250-8713, OR USE THE FORM ON PAGE 141.

Boot Factor 5 T-Shirt. Now _you_ can own a copy of the shirts worn by the authors during their research. Nifty four-hole design allows free movement of head, arms, and torso! Three sizes: medium, large, tub-o-lard (XL). An awesome gift! **$10.00**

Beer Games Poster. When reading a whole book is too darn much trouble, try our Beer Games poster. This huge (23" x 35"), full color print is a handy reference tool and a charming decoration for home or office. Describes over 20 of the most popular games, plus gaming rules and etiquette. **$10.00**

Boot Factor 5 Game Accessory. Created to celebrate the revised and expanded editions of our books, this unique barf bag is sturdy _and_ stylish! Using the same multi-ply construction as airline bags, our Game Accessory won't leak, burst, or spill—no matter how loudly you "yell for Europe." A party essential, especially if you have nice carpet. **20 bags for $10.00**

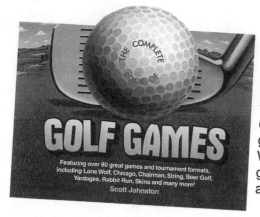

The Complete Book of Golf Games. Spice up your next round of 18 holes by playing these fun, challenging betting contests. Over 80 games—from Skins to Wolf to Beer Golf—plus great cartoons, trivia, and more! **$12.00**

Paintball! Strategies & Tactics. More fun than a round of Beer Hunter, paintball is one of the world's fastest growing sports. But there's more to the game than just running through the woods and shooting people with paint, and this book details both basic _and_ advanced tactical ideas that will give you and your team a competitive edge. Don't play without it! **$12.95**

Let's Blow thru Europe. Why spend hours in Europe touring dull museums and dusty cathedrals? _Blow 'em off!_ Instead, have a blast with this guide to the wildest bars, coolest restaurants, and hottest clubs. Part wicked satire, part practical guidebook, **Let's Blow** is your passport to a great time in Europe. **$12.95**

Order Form

MAIL TO: Mustang Publishing, PO Box 770426, Memphis, TN 38177 • USA
or call 800-250-8713 (or 901-684-1200) or fax 901-684-1256

Name _____

Address _____

City _____ State _____ Zip _____

Phone (_____) _____

QTY.	ITEM	TOTAL
_____	**The Complete Book of Beer Drinking Games** $8.95	$_____
_____	**Beer Games 2: The Exploitative Sequel** $8.95	$_____
_____	**The Hangover Handbook** $8.95	$_____
_____	**Boot Factor 5 T-Shirt** $10.00 *Circle size:* Med Large Tub-o-Lard (XL)	$_____
_____	**Beer Games Poster** $10.00	$_____
_____	**Boot Factor 5 Game Accessory** 20 bags for $10	$_____
_____	**The Complete Book of Golf Games** $12.00	$_____
_____	**Paintball! Strategies & Tactics** $12.95	$_____
_____	**Let's Blow thru Europe** $12.95	$_____

Shipping: 1-2 items, $3 per item; 3 or more, $2 per item $_____
For rush delivery (2-3 days), add $2.00 $_____
Orders outside the USA and Canada, add $5 for Air Mail $_____
Tennessee residents add 8.25% sales tax $_____

ORDER TOTAL $_____

Payment: check • money order • credit card (Visa, MC, AMEX, Discover)

Card # _____ Exp. Date _____

Signature _____

*Quantities are limited, and prices are subject to change. Our books are
also available in most bookstores. **Thank you for your order!***

B1

The Beer Index

Total domestic and imported beer sales
in the U.S. in 1993: **5,893,100,000 gallons**

≈

Estimated number of 12-ounce servings
of beer sold in the U.S. in 1993:
62,859,733,333

≈

Estimated number of beer drinkers
in the U.S.: **84,000,000**

≈

Number of breweries licensed
to operate in the U.S. in 1973: **76**
in 1983: **89**
in 1989: **215**
in 1993: **391**

≈

Number of jobs generated
by the beer industry: **49,000**

≈

Amount of money that beer generates each
year in the U.S. economy: **$167,500,000,000**

≈

Amount collected each year by local,
state, and federal governments
from the beer business: **$13,000,000,000**

Source: *Beer, the Magazine*

The Absolutely Final List of Synonyms for "Drunk"

beastly
beerified
pixillated
activated
antifreezed
winterized
varnished
stewed
afflicted
stuccoed
illuminated
inspired
in Mexico
on Olympus
on instruments
back-assward
baptized
getting there
fogmatic
gaga
Kentucky-fried
drunkulent
drinkative
bulletproof
besotted

feeling no pain
can't see through a ladder
under the affluence of incohol
zippered
upholstered
shipwrecked
popeyed
googly-eyed
irrigated
marinated
legless
fur-brained
beyond salvage
coagulated
ombalmed
incognito
liquorfied
mesmerized
overboard
tattooed
wallpapered
flusterated
fearless
certified
had it

YOU CAN HELP US FIND MORE DRINKING GAMES.

Or you can turn the page...

This is a picture of starving authors. They are starving because they don't have any more beer games to write about. Pathetic, aren't they?

But we know that you, a true gaming enthusiast, won't let them starve for long. We know that you will gladly share your knowledge of any obscure, hilarious games that the authors' extensive research efforts failed to uncover.

So, let us hear from you. If we use your game or suggestion in our next book, we'll send you a free, autographed copy! Of course, if we don't use your game, you'll just get on another mailing list and get tons of junk mail. Write to:

Mustang Publishing
Beer Research Dept.
P.O. Box 770426
Memphis, TN 38177 • USA

(All contributors will receive recognition in the book, as well as a free barf bag or something equally nice. Your contribution, which becomes the property of Mustang Publishing, is probably not tax deductible, but feel free to give it a shot anyway.)